3

EDEXCEL
CRIME
& PUNISHMENT THROUGH TIME
PLUS PROTEST

Donald Cumming

Joanne Philpott

DYNAMIC LEARNING

HODDER
EDUCATION
AN HACHETTE UK COMPANY

The authors and publishers would like to thank: Ian Dawson for the reuse of material from Crime and Punishment Through Time; Dale Banham for helping to create the Exam Busters feature; and Michael Riley for helping to plan the enquiry-based approach in the Protest Source Enquiry.

This material has been endorsed by Edexcel and offers high quality support for the delivery of Edexcel qualifications. Edexcel endorsement does not mean that this material is essential to achieve any Edexcel qualification, nor does it mean that this is the only suitable material available to support any Edexcel qualification. No endorsed material will be used verbatim in setting any Edexcel examination and any resource lists produced by Edexcel shall include this and other appropriate texts. While this material has been through an Edexcel quality assurance process, all responsibilty for the content remains with the publisher. Copies of official specifications for all Edexcel qualifications may be found on the Edexcel website www.edexcel.com.

The Schools History Project

Set up in 1972 to bring new life to history for students aged 13–16, the Schools History Project continues to play an innovatory role in secondary history education. From the start, SHP aimed to show how good history has an important contribution to make to the education of a young person. It does this by creating courses and materials which both respect the importance of up-to-date, well-researched history and provide enjoyable learning experiences for students.

Since 1978 the Project has been based at Trinity and All Saints University College Leeds. It continues to support, inspire and challenge teachers through the annual conference, regional courses and website: www.schoolshistoryproject.org.uk. The Project is also closely involved with government bodies and awarding bodies in the planning of courses for Key Stage 3, GCSE and A level.

Although every effort has been made to ensure that website addresses are correct at time of going to press, Hodder Education cannot be held responsible for the content of any website mentioned in this book. It is sometimes possible to find a relocated web page by typing in the address of the home page for a website in the URL window of your browser.

Hachette UK's policy is to use papers that are natural, renewable and recyclable products and made from wood grown in sustainable forests. The logging and manufacturing processes are expected to conform to the environmental regulations of the country of origin.

Orders: please contact Bookpoint Ltd, 130 Milton Park, Abingdon, Oxon OX14 4SB. Telephone: +44 (0)1235 827720. Fax: +44 (0)1235 400454. Lines are open 9.00a.m.–5.00p.m., Monday to Saturday, with a 24-hour message answering service. Visit our website at www.hoddereducation.co.uk.

© Donald Cumming and Joanne Philpott 2011
First published in 2011 by
Hodder Education,
an Hachette UK company
338 Euston Road
London NW1 3BH

Impression number   10 9 8 7 6 5 4 3 2
Year   2015   2014   2013

Typeset in 11/13 pt Palatino Light
Layouts by Lorraine Inglis Design
Artwork by Dylan Gibson, Barking Dog, Steve Smith, Peter Lubach and Richard Duszczak
Printed and bound in Dubai

A catalogue record for this title is available from the British Library

ISBN 978 0 340 99134 3

Contents

Before you start using this book here is a guide to help
you get the most out of it.

Enquiries

The book is structured around a series of Enquiries, each
one focusing on a key aspect of your GCSE course.
Each Enquiry helps you understand a particular event,
person or breakthrough and then links it to the
broader history of crime and punishment.

Banners introduce each Enquiry so you know exactly what you
are focusing on from the start.

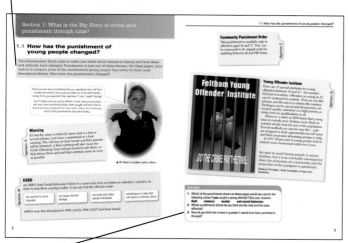

Activities guide you through the material so you build up your
knowledge and understanding of the key content of your
GCSE course. They also link into the on-going Smarter
Revision activities.

Meet the Examiner

These pages explain how to win high marks in your
examinations. They show you how to:

- answer each type of question in your examinations
- identify exactly what a question is asking
- structure answers and develop your vocabulary to
  make full use of what you know.

Dynamic Learning

Dynamic Learning provides an extensive range of
supporting resources:

- Enquiries developing your knowledge and
  understanding of key topics within each period
- Thematic investigations on major themes across time
- Extension activities to expand your knowledge
- Decision-making activities on key issues.

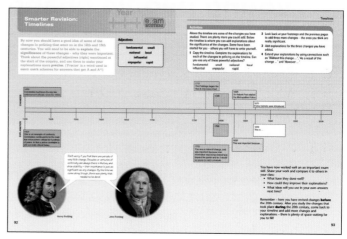

Smarter Revision

These pages help you prepare effectively for your
examinations, showing you a variety of ways to build
up your knowledge and understanding of the history
of crime and punishment. You will be building up your
revision material from the very beginning of your
course – not waiting until you have completed it. See
page 8 for more details on Smarter Revision pages.

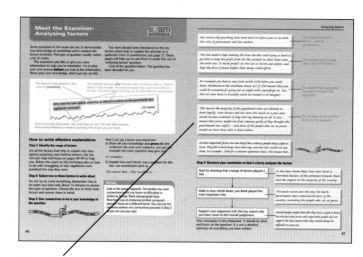

Sample answers help you identify what makes a good answer.

1.1 How has the punishment of young people changed?

This Development Study aims to make you think about themes in history and how ideas and attitudes have changed. Punishment is just one of these themes. On these pages, your task is to compare some of the punishments young people face today to those used throughout history. How have the punishments changed?

> Have you ever done something that you regretted later on? Said something hurtful? Lied to get yourself out of trouble? Stolen money from your parents? Ever had that 'if only I hadn't' feeling?
>
> I am PC Ward and, as a police officer, I meet many young people who have done something foolish, been caught and then had to face a serious punishment for their crime. Allow me to show you some of the punishments they face today.

Option A

Warning

If I feel the crime is relatively minor and is a first or second offence, I can issue a reprimand or a final warning. This will stay on their record and their parents will be informed. A final warning will also mean the Youth Offending Team will get involved with them, to help reform them and end their criminal career as soon as possible.

▲ PC Ward, a modern police officer.

Option B

ASBO

An ASBO (Anti-Social Behaviour Order) is a court order that sets limits on offenders' activities, in order to stop them causing trouble. It can say that the offender must:

not use foul or racist language	not cause criminal damage	not meet with other named individuals	not behave in a way that will alarm or distress others

ASBOs were first introduced in 1999, and by 2006 12,675 had been issued.

Community Punishment Order

This punishment is available only to offenders aged 16 and 17. They can be sentenced to do unpaid work for anything between 40 and 240 hours.

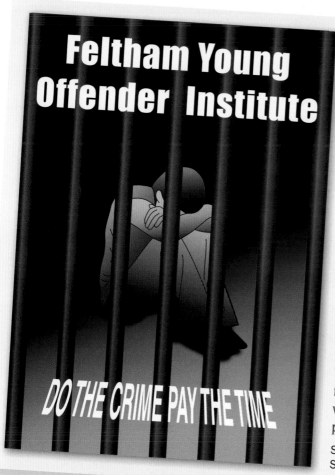

Feltham Young Offender Institute

DO THE CRIME PAY THE TIME

Young Offender Institute

There are 17 special institutes for young offenders between 15 and 17 – for example Feltham in London. Offenders as young as 12 can be sentenced to custody. They are run like prisons, and the aim is to reform the inmates. Privileges can be earned and all prisoners are treated equally; education is a high priority as many have no qualifications at all.

However, a study in 2004 found that young men in custody were 18 times more likely to commit suicide than the rest of the population. Several methods are used to stop this – cells are designed to limit opportunities to self harm, and there are posters advertising services to help.

In 1997, 80 per cent of young people held in custody were reconvicted within two years.

We want to avoid having people in secure facilities, but it is an inevitable consequence when the protection of a community and the protection of the youngster is paramount.

Stephen Pilkington, Chief Constable of Avon and Somerset.

Activities

1 Which of the punishments shown on these pages would you use for the following crimes if **you** caught a young offender? Give your reasons.
   theft   **violence**   **murder**   **anti-social behaviour**
2 Which punishments shown do you think are the most and the least effective?
3 How do you think the crimes in question 1 would have been punished in the past?

The Big Story of crime and punishment through time

Of course, the punishments shown on pages 2–3 have not always been used throughout history. Take a look at the punishments on these two pages from the past few centuries and think about how they compare to those today.

- Are punishments more lenient now, or are they harsher?
- Can you explain the reasons behind the punishments?

Harsh   **Lenient**

Activities

Read the three boxes on pages 4–5 carefully. Work in a group of three. You have to give a one-minute presentation answering the question 'How has the punishment of young people changed through time?' You should also think about *why* the different punishments were used. Use the following steps to help you to prepare your answer:

Step 1

Evaluate the punishments on pages 4–5. Where would you place these punishments on the historical scale – are they lenient or harsh?

Step 2

Repeat step 1, looking at the punishments on pages 2–3.

Step 3

How would you sum up how the punishment of young offenders has changed?

Step 4

Think about why we punish criminals:
a) To **deter** would-be criminals from committing crime.
b) To **compensate** victims and make them feel better.
c) To protect society by **removing** the criminals.
d) To take **revenge** against the criminals.
e) To **reform** the criminals and make them useful members of society.

For each punishment shown on pages 2–5, explain which of the reasons above is behind the punishment.

Execution

In the 18th century young people committing minor crimes like stealing could be executed. Here are just two examples:
- **18 September 1765** Elizabeth Gould, aged 16, was sentenced to death for stealing £20 (roughly £1,500 in modern money).
- **24 October 1787** James Shirley, aged 17, was sentenced to death for stealing a horse.

OLD BAILEY COURTHOUSE, LONDON

7 January 1850

Henry Whitehouse, aged 18, was sentenced to 6 months in jail for stealing a coat and some small items.

James Bennett, aged 17, was sentenced to 14 days in jail for stealing one loaf of bread.

John White, aged 16, was sentenced to one year in jail for stealing a saw. He had a previous conviction for theft.

Prisons

Until 1908, young people generally faced the same punishments as adults. For example, they went to the same prisons as adults.

Borstal

- In 1902 the first borstal was opened. These were youth prisons aimed at reforming offenders under the age of 21, and allowed separation of the young from adult criminals.
- The regime was strict and there was a great deal of discipline, though there is little evidence of corporal punishments like whipping. However caning was used in Approved Schools, a similar punishment to borstal.
- Education and exercise were key parts of borstal life.
- Borstals were discontinued in 1982.

A blacksmith's workshop at a borstal, 1945. Borstal boys were taught a trade, so they could earn an honest living when they were released. ▶

1.2 New crimes or new versions of old crimes?

You have seen an overview of changing punishments, and the reasons behind them. But what about crimes? On these pages you will be asked to think about change and continuity, in particular the changes and continuities in those activities we call 'crimes'.

Have the same things always been seen as crimes? Or have some new crimes developed over the centuries, while others have stopped being crimes? You will investigate this in greater detail later in this book, but for now consider this question:

Have there been any new crimes in the 20th century or are they all simply new variations of old crimes?

To answer this effectively you will need to balance change and continuity, and make an overall decision about just how far things have changed.

Key word

Continuity – little or no change

Activities

1 Work in pairs. Look at the crimes below. You have to decide if each modern crime is
a) a brand new crime or
b) a new version of an old crime.
You will explain your decisions to the rest of the class.

2 Draw up a list of any **other** modern crime you can think of. Discuss with your partner – are there any equivalent crimes from previous centuries they could be matched to or are they new crimes?

Modern crimes

Online fraud is increasing as more people use the internet.

Sex discrimination is now illegal.

Carjacking – holding motorists up at gunpoint and robbing them.

Forging money was a crime punishable by death.

Highway robbery was a concern in the 18th century.

Old crimes

Women who killed their husbands could be burnt at the stake.

3 Now you have discussed your thoughts ... where do you think the balance lies? Has there been mainly **change** – lots of new crimes – or has there been mainly **continuity** – new versions of old crimes? Explain your conclusion to your learning partner by finishing the sentences on the right:

As I have shown, there was mainly ...

The most significant change was ...

As a result ...

Why do most people think crime is much worse than it actually is?
Read the headlines below. They should give you a clue:

Another teenager stabbed to death

Boy shot in park highlights Britain's growing problem with gun crime

RIPPER BRUTALLY MURDERS ANOTHER VICTIM

Notorious villainies that are now practised in the kingdom

Explaining why

One answer is the influence of the media – newspapers, books, television and the internet. In fact, people who read the exaggerated stories in tabloid newspapers are twice as likely to worry about crime than those who read broadsheet newspapers. People have always been interested in reading stories about crime, the more shocking the better.

As you will come to see in this book, the influence of the media has been an important factor influencing people's attitudes to crime and punishment at different times over the last 2,000 years.

Factors influencing crime

Here are a group of people you are going to meet regularly during the course. They are the reasons, the **factors**, which explain the changes and continuities in crime and punishment, and the attitudes to crimes!

There are nine factors. Sometimes two or more work together. Sometimes a factor doesn't apply at all. But you'll find they all affect what happens to crime and punishment right through the course so it's worth remembering them. You will be reminded to look for factors many times and whenever you see this 'factor' wheel there will be an activity to focus on finding 'factors' at work.

FACTOR WHEEL

Roles of governments · Attitudes and beliefs · Media · Urbanisation (the growth of towns) · Poverty and wealth · Key individuals · Transport and communications · Science and technology · Religion · Economic and social conditions

Activities

1 Which of the factors do you think might cause an increase in crime?
2 Which of them might help to reduce crime?
3 How might each factor lead to changes in punishment?

7

What are the best ways to prepare for your GCSE exams?

Good revision and planning will help you do well at GCSE. We will help you through the two important features below.

 smarter revision

The Smarter Revision toolkit

The toolkit will help you prepare your revision notes thoroughly and intelligently.
Each tool helps you with a different aspect of your revision.
The page numbers show you where to find full explanations.

Living graph – helps you see the pattern of change and continuity in each theme. See page 9.

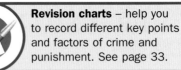
Revision charts – help you to record different key points and factors of crime and punishment. See page 33.

Timeline – helps you to see the pattern of change and continuity in each theme. See page 92.
 Year

SMARTER REVISION TOOLKIT

 FACTOR
Concept map – helps you to link factors to improve your explanation. See page 98.

Memory map – a very visual way to help you to remember the key developments in a period. See page 28.

 Hello cheeky!
Mnemonics – a fun way to help you to remember key points for your exam answers. See page 29.

 meet the examiner

These pages will:

a) advise you how to write good answers **and** how to avoid writing bad answers

b) show you sample answers and ask you to mark and improve them

c) set you sample questions to improve your skills at writing good answers.

Over the last few pages you have looked at a lot of information in text form; but have you considered turning it into a graph? Graphs like this are really helpful for following the story of crime and punishment across time so it's important to start early – and that means NOW!

Activities

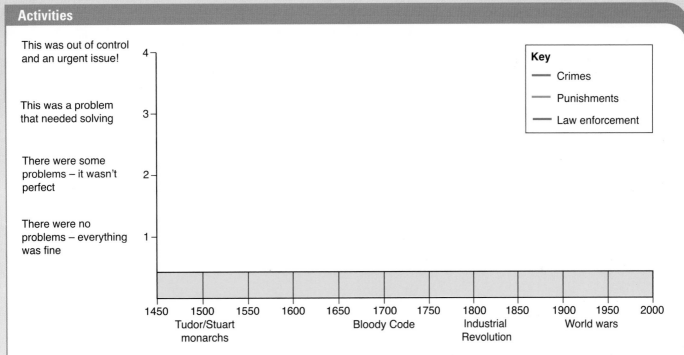

This was out of control and an urgent issue!

This was a problem that needed solving

There were some problems – it wasn't perfect

There were no problems – everything was fine

Key
— Crimes
— Punishments
— Law enforcement

1450 1500 1550 1600 1650 1700 1750 1800 1850 1900 1950 2000

Tudor/Stuart monarchs   Bloody Code   Industrial Revolution   World wars

You will need to study pages 12–17 before you can complete this task.

You are going to create three lines on your graph.

1 Work in a small group. Choose one theme:
   a) crimes
   b) punishments
   c) law enforcement.
2 Use the Criminal Moments in Time on pages 12–17 (and your own Criminal Moment in Time for the 21st century).
   a) Pick out from each picture the information about your theme. Decide for each date where to place your theme on the graph. (For example, if you think crime in 1450 was out of control and an urgent issue put a cross at level 4 above 1450).
   b) Use sticky notes to list the evidence for your decision about the level. Stick these on your graph.

3 When your outline graph is complete you have one minute to explain it aloud to the rest of the class. You must include each of these words:
   • continuity   • change   • attitudes.
   Repeat steps 2 and 3 for the other two themes in step 1.
4 Compare the lines for each theme. What similarities and differences can you see between the shapes of the three lines?
5 Look back at the information about punishments for young offenders on pages 2–5.
   a) Add this as a new line on the graph – you will have to think carefully about your decisions as some of the information may be contradictory.
   b) Discuss this line with the rest of your group. What key words should you include aside from the ones in step 3?
   c) How do the factors you have already met on page 7 explain some of these changes?

Meet the Examiner: Introducing the Development Study exam

Unit 1: Development Study – Crime and Punishment

This unit is assessed by a 1 hour 15 minute exam. The exam paper below gives you an idea what the exam for Unit 1 looks like. We have not included

Sources A and B for Question 1. In the exam paper, Questions 3, 4, 5b and 6b will have accompanying stimulus material that you are allowed to use. We have not included this here.

Unit 1: Development Study – Crime and Punishment
Time: 1 hour 15 minutes

Answer Questions 1 and 2, **EITHER** Question 3 **OR** 4 then **EITHER** Question 5(a) and 5(b) **OR** 6(a) and 6(b).
The total mark for this paper is 50.

①

Answer Question 1 AND Question 2.

1 What can you learn from Sources A and B about changes in punishment between the Middle Ages and the 19th century? **(4 marks)**

2 The boxes below show two important individuals.

② Choose **one** individual and explain why that person was important in changing attitudes towards law enforcement. **(9 marks)**

| Robert Peel and the police | Jonathan Wild, the Thief-Taker General |

Answer EITHER Question 3 OR Question 4.

EITHER

③ 3 Why did prisons change so much in the 19th century? **(12 marks)**

OR

4 Why were the laws against poaching so difficult to enforce in the 17th and 18th centuries? **(12 marks)**

Answer EITHER Question 5 OR Question 6.
You must answer both parts of the question you choose.

EITHER

5 **Crime and punishment from Roman Britain to c.1450.**

④ (a) Describe the key features of law and order in Roman times. **(9 marks)**

(b) How much did the system of law and order change from the Anglo-Saxon period to the Norman period? Explain your answer. **(16 marks)**

⑤

OR

6 **Changing views of the nature of criminal activity c.1450 to present day.**

(a) Describe the key features of the laws to do with domestic violence after 1970. **(9 marks)**

(b) How different was the way the crime of witchcraft was treated in the 16th century compared to the 18th century? **(16 marks)**

Thinking for success

TIMING AND MARKS

The marks for **each** question are shown in brackets. Use this as a guide as to how much time to spend on each question.

It is important to time yourself carefully. Some students run out of time because they spend too long on the first two questions. These questions are worth a **total** of 13 marks. The higher marks come later so keep a close eye on your timings:

- Questions 1 AND 2: 20 minutes
- Question 3 OR 4: 15 minutes
- Question 5 OR 6: 35 minutes (aim to spend at least 20 minutes on part (b), as this carries the most marks).

This leaves 5 minutes to check your answers.

FOLLOW INSTRUCTIONS CAREFULLY

Read the instructions very carefully. You must answer Questions 1 and 2, but notice that for Question 2 you choose **one** example to write about. If you write about both examples you will not gain extra marks, but you will waste valuable time!

THINK CAREFULLY ABOUT WHICH QUESTION YOU CHOOSE

After Questions 1 and 2 you need to make TWO important choices.

Choice 1

You need to decide whether to answer Question 3 or Question 4. This will test your knowledge of material in Sections 3 and 4 of this book.

Choice 2

You need to decide whether to answer Question 5 or Question 6. These are set on the two 'Extension Units'. You will probably study only one of these extension units so make sure you know which one to answer in the exam!

Question 5 will be on **Crime and punishment from Roman Britain to c.1450** (see Section 2).

Question 6 will be on **Changing views of the nature of criminal activity c.1450 to present day** (see Section 6).

Types of questions

There may be a difference between the types of questions presented here and on the exam paper, and where they appear on the exam paper.

1 **INFERENCE QUESTIONS**
The first question will usually be an inference question. It may ask you to think about attitudes to crimes. You will need to use both sources to answer this question. You will find advice about this type of question on page 135.

2 **'ANALYSIS OF IMPORTANCE' QUESTIONS**
This question asks you to explain why an event/individual was important, and its impact on Crime and Punishment. The Exam Busters on pages 80–81 help you to answer this type of question effectively.

3 **'ANALYSIS OF FACTORS' QUESTIONS**
Some questions ask you to explain why something happened, analysing the factors involved. This type of question usually carries

a lot of marks. You have already been introduced on page 7 to the factors which explain the changes and continuities in crime and punishment. The Exam Busters on pages 46–47 help you to tackle 'factors' questions effectively.

4 **'KEY FEATURES' QUESTIONS**
This type of question asks you to show/demonstrate your precise knowledge of a particular law or crime. The Exam Busters on pages 116–117 explain how to approach this type of question.

5 **'ANALYSIS AND EVALUATION' QUESTIONS**
Some questions require a longer answer. You need to analyse and **evaluate** a punishment or a crime. The exam paper will give you three hints – but it is always best to plan your answer before reading them. The Exam Busters on pages 110–111 help you with this type of question.

Criminal Moment in Time 1: London, 1450

Let us start your investigations with a look at the year 1450, before you move forward in time. This is the start of the core study of your course. Look carefully at the picture and see what you can learn about:

- crimes
- punishments
- law enforcement.

Activities

1 What evidence can you find in this picture of 1450 about:

 a) methods of law enforcement

 b) methods of punishment

 c) the sorts of crimes being committed?

2 What adjectives would you use to describe the legal system and crimes in 1450? Do you think the legal system was effective?

3 After 1476 the printing press was used in England, and pamphlets spreading news of crimes were read by people. Fear of crime also increased. Can you think why this might have happened?

The constable was the local law enforcement officer. This was an unpaid position that any man could be asked to do.

Coroners would be called if there was a suspicious death.

Towns were rare and most people still lived in small villages, where everyone knew each other. Local communities were responsible for law and order, and for their own poor.

The army was used to stop riots and protests.

If you could recite Psalm 51 of the Bible you could claim 'benefit of clergy' and escape punishment by the courts. In the 1500s monarchs stopped this loophole for most serious crimes.

Religious beliefs meant that gambling and other sinful activities were increasingly outlawed.

Piracy and theft from ships was a crime punishable by death.

I've had my pig stolen!

Quick, raise the hue and cry!

I hope the constable comes soon!

I'll still have to get the evidence myself.

In 1476 the first printing press was set up in London. Soon stories about vagabonds and witches were being published, which led to an increasing fear of crime.

Prisons were privately run and prisoners could buy whatever they could afford to make life there more comfortable.

Traitors really lost their heads!

There is a public hanging of some thieves tomorrow – town is bound to be busy!

Monarchs made sure any protests were dealt with severely and body parts were sent around the country as a deterrent.

In a trial the decision about guilt was taken by a jury made up of local men. They looked at the evidence and the character of the person to make their decision.

Public punishments were used to humiliate criminals and to deter others from committing crimes.

BOOKS

TAVERN

COUNTY GAOL

13

Criminal Moment in Time 2: Portsmouth, 1750

Now travel forward in time to 1750 to find out how much and how quickly things changed. Remember you are looking out for changes in:

- crimes
- punishments
- law enforcement.

Activities

1 What evidence can you find in this picture of 1750 of continuities in:

   a) methods of law enforcement

   b) methods of punishment

   c) the sorts of crimes being committed?

2 What changes can you see in any aspect of crime and punishment?

3 What adjectives would you use to describe the degree of difference between 1450 and 1750?

4 In the late 1700s crime rates began to increase. Can you think why this might have happened?

I'm in here because I owe money – and can't afford to pay to get out!

Watchmen were employed in towns to patrol the streets both day and night. But they were poorly paid and of little use.

Times have changed. Soon I'll not be able to carry out my crime!

Poverty meant people often broke the law to survive.

Criminal Moment in Time 3: London, 1845

Now travel forward in time to 1845 to find out how much and how quickly things changed. Remember you are looking out for changes in:

- crimes
- punishments
- law enforcement.

Activities

1 What evidence can you find in this picture of 1845 of continuities in:

   a) methods of law enforcement

   b) methods of punishment

   c) the sorts of crimes being committed?

2 What changes can you see in any aspect of crime and punishment?

3 What adjectives would you use to describe the degree of difference between 1750 and 1845?

4 Create your own 'Criminal Moment in Time' for the 21st century. How much has changed?

16

The Industrial Revolution

The story of crime reflects the story of what else was happening in Britain at the time. In the years after 1750, Britain became the first country in the world to industrialise. It changed the lives of everyone in the country. It was a real revolution.

Prisons became an important form of punishment. Prisoners either worked in silence or were kept separate from each other. They were given religious instruction. The authorities hoped that this would help them reform.

The government took an active role in running prisons and the police.

Faster transport made it easier for criminals to get away.

The judge listened to the evidence and decided that I should pay a fine of 10 shillings for stealing the piece of bread.

Royal judges visited counties four times a year. They were experts in the law. They judged serious crimes. At the royal courts, a jury was still used.

How are we going to pay? We can't afford to eat.

Large numbers of convicts were transported to Australia.

COURT HOUSE

PRISON

STATION

THIRD FIRST

SIMMONS UNDERTAKER
CARPENTRY & JOINERY

BLOGGS FRUIT & WINE IMPORTERS

Section 2: How much did crime and punishment change from Roman Britain to *c.*1450?

2.1 How did the Romans try to prevent crime?

When you think of the Romans today you probably think about straight roads and conquering armies. And it was the conquering armies that led to an empire stretching from the Middle East all the way to the cold island of Britannia! But was it the armies that helped them to prevent crime? This enquiry helps you to decide.

Activity

Your task is to investigate Roman law and order, using the information from pages 18–21 and your own research. You should produce an exhibition display showing the key features of:

- Roman laws and trials
- Roman policing
- Roman punishments
- the attitudes behind the laws.

Source 1

The Roman legal writer Ulpian said that the governor of a province such as Britain had a duty to 'see that the province is peaceful and quiet. This will not be difficult, if he acts diligently to search for wicked men and to remove them from the province; he must search for temple-robbers, brigands, kidnappers, thieves and punish anyone committing these offences.'

Historians think that the same basic laws applied across the empire – though they cannot be 100 per cent certain. Source 1 shows us that maintaining law and order was an important part of daily life across the Roman Empire.

Written laws

The Romans used standard written laws, which were displayed in towns, to make sure citizens knew what activities were not allowed. The 'twelve tablets' were the first recorded Roman laws in 450BC; in AD533 the Institutes of Justinian were written down. These were a more detailed record of all Roman laws. The basic rules included:

ANY ROMAN CITIZEN COULD BRING A CASE TO COURT

THE DEFENDANT WAS INNOCENT UNTIL PROVED GUILTY

THE DEFENDANT HAD THE RIGHT TO PRESENT EVIDENCE

DEFENDANTS HAD A RIGHT TO A FAIR AND OPEN TRIAL

Trials: Minor crime

At the magistrates' court a judge was chosen (he was not a lawyer, although he could take advice from lawyers) and both sides presented their evidence. Then the judge reached his decision. In parts of the empire such as Britain, centurions could be used in the place of magistrates if the crime was very minor.

Trials: Serious crime

There was a slightly different system for more serious cases like murder. Cases were tried by magistrates but this time with a jury. Again, anyone could bring a case to court for trial. When the suspect appeared, both sides gave evidence and then the jury decided if he or she was guilty. The magistrate then decided the sentence. In places like Britain the Roman governor would take up this role.

Roman policing

In the early years of the Roman Empire there was no police force. If a Roman was attacked or robbed he had to rely on friends and neighbours to catch the attacker or thief. This often led to more violence.

In AD6 Emperor Augustus set up three kinds of forces to police Rome (see below). However, the situation there did not change much. Most were occupied with fire fighting. The core of the police were riot troops.

The forces of law and order in Rome from c.AD6 to c.AD400

Praetorian guard

The Emperor's household guard was used only in emergencies to protect the Emperor from riots.

Urban cohorts

There were 3,000 urban cohorts. They were soldiers. Their main job was to keep order by stopping riots. They did not patrol the streets.

The vigiles

There were 7,000 vigiles. Their main duty was preventing and putting out fires. On patrol at night they tried to stop crimes or capture runaway slaves.

Rebellions

It was the job of the Governor of Britain to stop rebellions. In 118AD, Quintus Pompeius Falco was governor and had to put down rebellions by several tribes across northern England and Scotland – he used the Roman army to do this.

Do-it-yourself!

Stealing was regarded as a minor crime because it did not affect the ruler or the majority of the people. You had to find the criminal yourself. You had to collect the evidence yourself. You had to take the accused to court yourself. It was not the job of the police to do any of this!

Roman policing in Britain

In far-flung parts of the empire such as Britain the army took on the role of policing the villages and towns. The Roman army included Britons as well as men from across the Empire.

Source 2

Translation

I implore your mercifulness not to allow me, a man from overseas and an innocent one, about whose good faith you may inquire, to have been bloodied by rods as if I had committed some crime.

▲ This source is by a civilian at Vindolanda Fort on Hadrian's Wall. He was asking the Roman military governor not to punish him. What does this suggest about the role the army had in law and order?

Were snakes really used as punishments?

Christians being thrown to the lions is a punishment we have all heard of. But were punishments as harsh as this might suggest? And what does that tell us about Roman society? These pages show you some examples of the punishments the Romans used, and the attitudes that lay behind them.

Activities

1 Continue your investigation from page 18.
2 What can you learn about Roman Britain compared to the rest of the Roman Empire?

Attitudes to punishment

This imaginary scene shows some Roman senators discussing why they think harsh punishments should be used.

Source 1

The Roman historian, Tacitus, described the fighting in *The Annals of Imperial Rome*.

In AD59 there was a serious fight between the people of two Roman towns, Nuceria and Pompeii. It began at a gladiatorial show. Both sides shouted taunts at each other; then the abuse led to stone throwing and then swords were drawn. The people of Pompeii, where the show was held, came off better. Many Nucerians were wounded. Many died, leaving bereaved parents and children.

We must make sure trials are fair so the guilty are properly convicted.

We have a large empire and the punishments need to send a clear message to everyone.

The more violent an execution is, the better. It will frighten others away from crime.

Prisons are expensive. Who will pay the gaolers?

At least executions are cheap.

We cannot afford more guards on the street. Where will the money come from to pay them?

If we raise more taxes the people may riot. It's not our job to tackle social problems.

Punishments for citizens (ordinary Romans)

Citizens could be put to death for serious crimes such as:

arson

attacking the Emperor

robbing temples

stealing farm animals

Punishment for minor crimes such as theft or selling under-weight bread included:

whipping

repaying the cost of goods

confiscation of property

Punishments for nobles

Nobles could be sentenced to death for serious crimes but they were allowed to go into exile and avoid prosecution.

Punishments for slaves

All the slaves in a household were crucified if one of them murdered or tried to murder their master.

Slaves could give evidence at a trial, but only if they had been tortured first!

Punishments for legionaries

Legionaries who ran away in battle faced execution. In addition, one in every ten men from the legion that they ran away from was chosen by lot and also executed. This decimation was carried out ruthlessly.

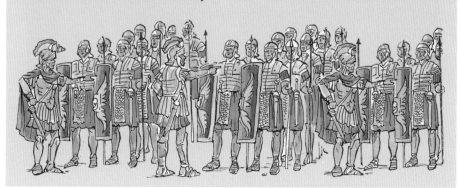

Roman punishments

Men, women, slaves and non-citizens all received different levels of punishment.

Prison sentences were not used as punishments by the Romans; only people in debt or who were awaiting trial or execution were in jail.

However, violent punishments were common. Anyone convicted of patricide (killing his father) was tied in a sack of snakes and thrown into the river to drown!

Over time Roman punishments became more violent. Extreme examples included execution by pouring molten lead down the throat and crucifixion for anyone who refused to recognise the Emperor as a god.

After Jews rebelled against Rome, one million were killed and thousands were transported to fight as gladiators.

After the slave revolt led by Spartacus 6,000 captured prisoners were crucified along the main road to Rome.

Activity

How do the punishments on this page support the claim that Roman punishments were harsh?

Exile

Some Romans were actually sent **to** Britain as a punishment – one example was Valentinus, a Roman governor who was exiled in 369AD to Britain as an alternative to execution. This shows us Roman attitudes to Britain!

2.2 How effective were laws in 'Dark Age' England?

The period from AD450 to 1066 is known by several names: The Dark Ages, Anglo-Saxon England and Early Medieval England. You, and the examiner, could choose any of these!

The centuries after the Romans left are sometimes called the Dark Ages, as evidence is hard to find and historians have sometimes thought that society became less organised and civilised. At first there were several small kingdoms, but by the 11th century England was one country with one king. But is it really the case that it became less organised? Your enquiry is to investigate the information and decide how effective the laws were, especially when compared to the harsh system of Roman Britain.

Activities

1 Read the information on pages 22–25 and copy and complete the table below. For each heading, record the evidence.

	Evidence of changes – very different to Romans	Evidence of continuity – little or no change
Laws and trials		
Policing		
Punishments		
The attitudes behind the laws		

2 Add explanations to your table. The sentence 'This suggests change/ continuity because ...' may help you. You could use sticky notes to add your explanations.
3 Overall does the evidence suggest there was mainly change or continuity between the Romans and the so-called 'Dark Ages'?

The King's Peace

An Anglo-Saxon king made all the important decisions about laws, with advice from the richest nobles in the country. Their job was to maintain the King's Peace, so that subjects could live without fear of crime. Capital punishment was not used as much, especially once the kings became Christian – instead they often used wergild (money given as compensation for victims) and mutilation (e.g. cutting off an ear) so criminals could repent of their sins and reform their ways.

Source 1

▲ An 11th-century manuscript showing the king as centre of decisions about law.

Source 2

6. If anyone steals anything in church he is to pay the normal fine and then have his hand struck off.

9. If a pregnant woman is murdered the killer is to pay the full wergild for the woman and half for the child.

19. If anyone lends his weapon to another so that he may kill a man he is to pay a third of the wergild.

23. If a dog bites or tears a man to death the owner is to pay 6 shillings for the first offence, on a second occasion 12 shillings.

40. If anyone neglects the rules of the Church in Lent he is to pay 120 shillings.

◀ Some of the laws of King Alfred the Great, ruler of the Kingdom of Wessex. These were written down in the 9th century so that everyone knew what was and wasn't a crime, although not all crimes were covered.

Tithings

There was no police force in England in this period. Instead, local communities relied on each other to catch thieves and wrongdoers. By the 10th century a system of tithings had been set up – what effect would there be if you had this system in your school?

Key features of a tithing

- All males over 12 belonged to a tithing.
- There were 10 males per tithing.
- If a member of a tithing broke the law it was the responsibility of the others to bring him to court – they had to raise a 'hue and cry' to alert the village.
- If they did not do this, all the other members had to pay compensation to the victim.

Trials by jury

In a trial the decision about guilt was still taken by a jury. There were no lawyers, just the people involved.

The jury was made up of local men who probably knew both the victim and the defendant, and would use their personal knowledge to help make their decision if there was no clear evidence.

The accused could swear an oath that they were innocent, if they had the support of character witnesses who would swear that they believed their oath. This was called *compurgation*.

If the jury could not agree, or if the accused could not find people willing to be their *compurgators*, then trial by ordeal (see page 24) was used.

Hundred Courts met each month. These were local courts for minor crime. All freemen had to attend and swear oaths to keep the peace.

Shire Courts met twice a year to deal with serious crime. Landowners and one person from every village attended these.

Royal Courts were where the king dealt with cases involving nobles and serious crimes.

If you did not attend court you were considered an outlaw and could be killed by anyone!

Trial by ordeal

If a jury could not decide if a defendant was guilty then it was handed over to God to make a decision. People were very religious and believed that God would reveal his decision through an ordeal. Religion was a key part of medieval life, and influenced many laws.

There were different types of ordeal, but there was always a religious ritual before it happened. The defendant had to fast for three days, and hear a mass service in church. Most of the ordeals also took place inside a church, and were begun by a priest.

Activities

1 Read pages 24–25 and make your own revision cards on trial by ordeal and wergilds.

2 Work in pairs. One of you should answer the question: 'Describe the key features of the trial by ordeal system'. The other should answer the question: 'Describe the key features of the system of wergilds'.

3 Use the book to mark each other's answers. Add what has been missed out.

Trial by hot water

This was usually taken by men. The accused had to take a small object out of boiling water – this would not be easy. The arm was bandaged and three days later checked to see if it was healing. God would show the man's guilt or innocence this way.

Trial by cold water

An ordeal often used for slaves. The accused was tied up with a knot at the waist and lowered into water (a river or pond close to the church – the other three ordeals happened inside the church). If the knot sank below the water they were innocent; if it stayed above the water they were guilty!

Trial by consecrated bread

This ordeal was for priests. First they had to pray and swear an oath to God. Then they ate a small piece of barley bread and cheese that had been blessed. If they choked it was seen as a sign that they were guilty. This might seem like a lenient ordeal, but people believed God would punish lying priests severely and it was considered to be very accurate – like an early lie detector.

Trial by hot iron

This was usually taken by women. Before the ordeal a priest said these words: 'If you are innocent of this charge you may confidently receive his iron in your hand and the Lord, the just judge, will free you just as he snatched the three children from the burning fire.'

Then the accused had to carry a piece of red hot iron for three metres. Her hand was bandaged and then unwrapped three days later. If the wound was healing then God was clearly saying the woman was innocent. But if the wound was festering and not healing then God was saying she was guilty.

Source 2

◄ Medieval illustrations of trial by ordeal – which ordeals do they show?

Which ordeals do these illustrations show? How useful are these for finding out about trial by ordeal?

What were the key features of Early Medieval punishments?

One question you need to be able to answer is a 'key features' question. Here you will need to outline the main points – for example, of a punishment. You can be awarded up to nine marks based on the quality of your knowledge. To get top marks you need to show you understand the attitude behind the punishment and how it links to the punishment itself.

The blood feud

Early Saxon kings allowed the victims of crimes to punish the criminals themselves. If someone was murdered, the family had the right to track down and kill the murderer. This right was known as the *blood feud*.

Wergilds

The blood feud was abolished by later kings by the 9th century. Instead of this rather violent system, a form of compensation was developed where money was paid to victims – this money was called a wergild. This made further violence much less likely.

Different prices were paid for different crimes, and people of higher status 'cost' more. For example the wergild for killing a noble man was 300 shillings – 200 shillings more than for killing a freeman. Fines were also used for some minor crimes. If criminals could not pay the fine then they were sent into slavery. Historians are not certain about every wergild, as Source 1 shows.

Some serious crimes, such as treason and arson, still carried the death penalty. Executions might happen in a particular public place – a cwealm-stowas (which means 'killing ground'). Repeat offenders were also punished harshly, often by mutilation.

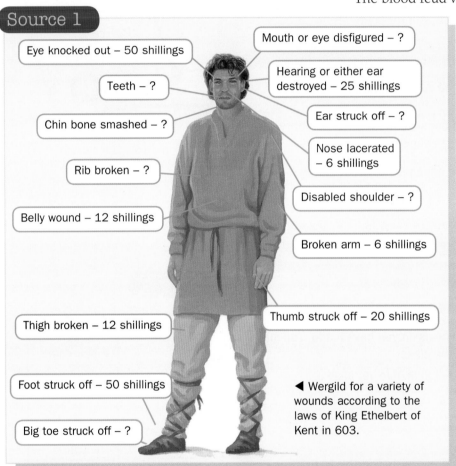

Source 1

- Eye knocked out – 50 shillings
- Mouth or eye disfigured – ?
- Teeth – ?
- Hearing or either ear destroyed – 25 shillings
- Chin bone smashed – ?
- Ear struck off – ?
- Nose lacerated – 6 shillings
- Rib broken – ?
- Disabled shoulder – ?
- Belly wound – 12 shillings
- Broken arm – 6 shillings
- Thigh broken – 12 shillings
- Thumb struck off – 20 shillings
- Foot struck off – 50 shillings
- Big toe struck off – ?

◀ Wergild for a variety of wounds according to the laws of King Ethelbert of Kent in 603.

Activity

4 The following crimes have been committed in the village. Use your knowledge of Medieval law and order to decide on the correct punishment for each one. You can choose from the list of selected punishments or use others you think are correct.

Crime	Punishment	Reason
Murder of a freeman		
Arson		
Assault in which tithing could not find the defendant		
Minor theft		

Possible punishments

Wergild   Fine   Execution   Mutilation   Slavery

2.3 How did crime and punishment change after 1066?

In 1066 England was conquered by the Norman duke William in the Norman Conquest. He now considered that all the land in the country belonged directly to him. The centuries that followed are known as the later Medieval period, and saw many changes to the way the country was run. But how much did crime and punishment actually change? And was there any continuity from the old systems?

Activities

Your job is to assess the *extent of change* in the centuries after the Norman Conquest.

1 Look at the information on these two pages, and for each category make a decision on the scale of change shown below.

	Continuity	(no change)		Great change
Categories	1	2	3	4
Laws and crimes				
Trials				
Punishments				
Policing				

2 Prepare a short explanation for each decision you have made. You may be asked to explain your decision to the class.

This category changed: _____. I think this because ...

Laws and crime

The king and his advisers passed laws. These included the hated forest laws – trees could not be chopped down for fuel and people living in forests could not own dogs. Anyone caught hunting deer would be executed.

Policing

Tithings were still used. From 1285 the hue and cry was developed: villagers had to organise themselves into a posse and chase criminals under the direction of the county sheriff.

Constables were introduced about 1250 – men responsible for law and order in their village. This unpaid job was held for only a year at a time.

Coroners and sheriffs had to investigate serious crime and bring the criminals to trial.

Justice
Evidence
Prison
Arrest
Police
Constable

▲ The language of the courts was changed to French and Latin. Modern English shows some of the French words still used today.

Crime	% of all major crime
Theft	73.5%
Murder	18.2%
Receiving stolen goods	6.2%
Arson	0.8%
Counterfeiting	0.6%
Rape	0.5%
Treason	0.2%

▲ This chart shows the categories of major crime committed in eight counties between 1300 and 1348. The number of thefts per person was actually much lower than it is today. Can you think why?

Trials

Trials by jury remained, as did trial by ordeal, for a few centuries. At first the new 'trial by combat' was introduced where God 'chose' the winning fighter to decide the outcome of a trial. However all trials by ordeal were ended in 1215.

In the 12th century a regular system of courts was established where royal judges travelled round the country to hear important cases. After 1361, landowners acted as 'Justices of the Peace' for minor crimes – an important local role.

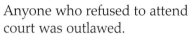

Punishments

In the 12th century, the death penalty and mutilation remained for serious crime and wergilds were ended. Fines were paid to the king's officials not to victims.

Anyone who refused to attend court was outlawed.

If you could read a verse from the Bible you would be tried in a Church Court instead of a Royal Court, where the punishments were lighter.

Executions took place in public to act as a deterrent.

The stocks, pillory and fines were often used for minor crimes.

Religion

A separate system of Church Courts was set up for priests. There was no capital punishment in Church Courts; this was called the 'benefit of clergy'. You could prove you were a priest by reading a verse from the Bible. The verse was known as the 'neck verse' because it saved your neck from being hanged! However, they did still use mutilation.

Criminals could also escape hanging by getting to a church and claiming sanctuary. This meant a criminal would be protected and could choose to be exiled from England instead of going on trial.

> Source 3

▲ This source shows the King's Bench Court in London – where the most serious crimes were put on trial. The criminals are at the bottom and the judges at the top beneath the King's arms. The jurors are on the left. Is this very different from a modern court?

> Source 4

▲ A sanctuary knocker from Durham Cathedral.

You're only just starting the course but we're thinking about helping you revise already. Revision isn't something you tack onto the end of a course. It's something you build up as you go – that makes it a lot easier. You are going to build one large memory map on medieval crime and punishment. That way it is already made to help you to revise later on in your course. How about that for saving time?

How can a map save you time and boost your memory?

- Memory maps encourage you to link pieces of information together. You learn more by making links, because it makes you think!

- You are actively involved with your revision. This is much better than simply reading, hoping your brain will act as a sponge and soak up the information!

- Your own images, colour and acronyms will help your memory. Psychologists have shown that the use of colour can help you remember over 50 per cent more information.

- Memory maps are a flexible tool for revision. You can produce a memory map from memory, check it against the original, then add in what you have missed.

- Finally, and perhaps most importantly, memory maps make revision a lot more interesting!

How to build your memory map

Step 1: Use plain A4 or, even better, A3 paper (landscape). Space is important. The end result should not look too busy or cramped.

Step 2: The memory map opposite shows you how you could start. Think of a central image that sums up the whole topic – it should be personal to you and doesn't have to be great art! Keep those branches curved – straight lines will limit the links you see later on.

Step 3: Look at your book and the pages on Medieval crime and add information to the map. A good use of colour would be to write Early Medieval information in one colour and Later Medieval information in another colour. Use pencils so that you can make any corrections that are needed later. Remember:

- Use key words or phrases. Do not write full sentences.

- Change the size of your writing as you add more branches.
  Start with big capitals and get smaller.

- Use pictures/images/diagrams/colour to replace or emphasise words. Many people find it easier to remember visual images than words.

▲ Example images – keep them simple!

Step 4: Read your map and look for links. Draw lines between ideas that are linked and write the explanation on the line. Good links to look for would be how much change there was in each area. Use the same rules as before – step 3 makes it clear.

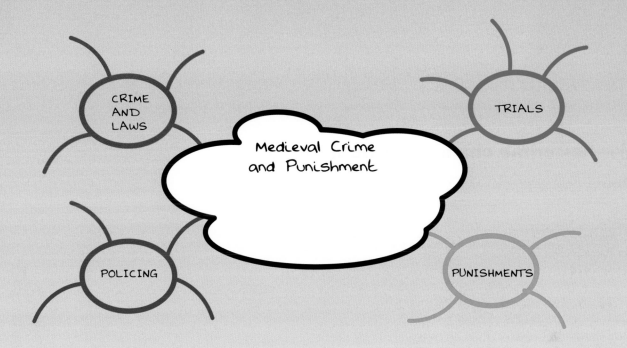

Using mnemonics

Mnemonics are a good example of fun revision – revision doesn't have to be boring. In fact it's difficult to learn anything if you're bored as you don't concentrate well. Inventing your own mnemonic can help you remember key pieces of information. The sillier the mnemonic the more likely you are to remember it.

This is an example of a very silly mnemonic to help you remember the different areas of change in crime and punishment during the Medieval period.

Cheeky = Crime

Tiny = Trials

Pink = Policing

Parrot = Punishments

It will help you to structure your answer in an exam – each one becomes a paragraph. The fact that it is silly means you will find it hard to forget! Suddenly all the information on your memory map will come flooding back to you.

What other mnemonics can you invent during your course?

In this section of your course you will investigate **crimes** and look at **why** the authorities criminalised certain activities by changing laws and **what attitudes** people had to these crimes.

How has crime changed through history?

This chart shows you an overview of crimes across time.

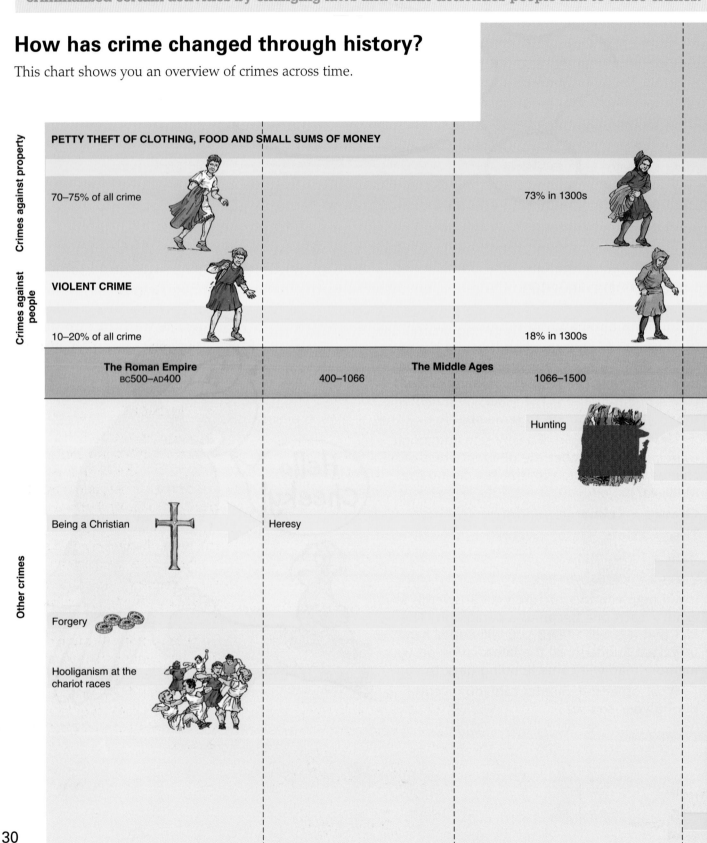

Crimes against property

PETTY THEFT OF CLOTHING, FOOD AND SMALL SUMS OF MONEY

70–75% of all crime

73% in 1300s

Crimes against people

VIOLENT CRIME

10–20% of all crime

18% in 1300s

The Roman Empire BC500–AD400	400–1066 **The Middle Ages**	1066–1500

Hunting

Other crimes

Being a Christian → Heresy

Forgery

Hooliganism at the chariot races

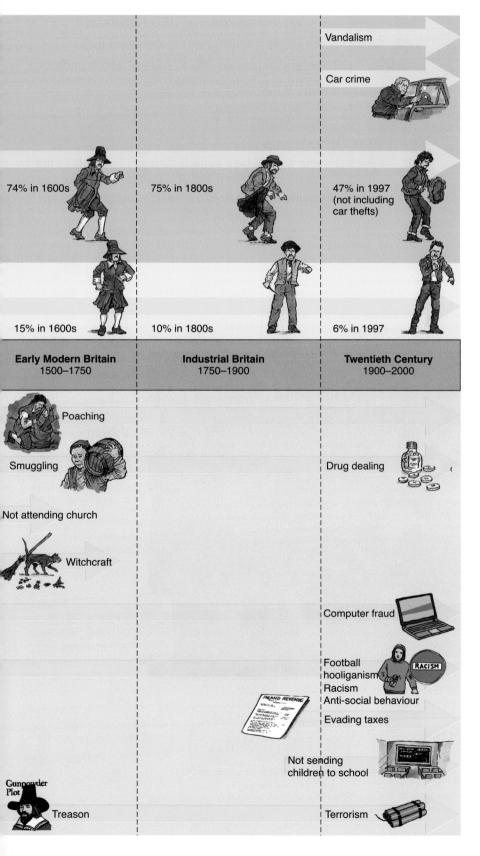

Vandalism

Car crime

74% in 1600s   75% in 1800s   47% in 1997
(not including
car thefts)

15% in 1600s   10% in 1800s   6% in 1997

Early Modern Britain 1500–1750	Industrial Britain 1750–1900	Twentieth Century 1900–2000

Poaching

Smuggling

Drug dealing

Not attending church

Witchcraft

Computer fraud

Football
hooliganism
Racism
Anti-social behaviour

Evading taxes

Not sending
children to school

Gunpowder
Plot

Treason

Terrorism

Activities

1 What patterns can you see in this chart? Work in pairs. You have one minute to describe the patterns to your partner. You should use the following keywords when talking about the chart:
   • change
   • continuity
   • minor crime
   • violent crime.
2 How different are modern crimes from old crimes?
3 The 'dark figure' in crime statistics is crime we have no records of. How does this affect the reliability of our conclusions?

The big ideas

1 There is a great deal of **continuity** in types of crime across time – **minor crimes** like theft dominate, and **violent crime** has actually declined.

2 New laws make new crimes – and these **changes** can make it seem like crime has gone up.

3 **Fear of crime** has often been greater than the level of crime justified.

4 Unreported crime: Because of the **dark figure** of unreported and unrecorded crime, we cannot be certain just how much crime there actually was. Even today, not every crime is reported and recorded.

31

3.1 What caused the rise and fall of highway robbery?

Some crimes are unusual. They grow suddenly, cause fear and alarm, then equally suddenly they seem to die out. Highway robbery, which peaked in the 18th century and which was punishable with death, is one of these crimes. Highwaymen could ride up to their victims, rob them at gunpoint and quickly ride off into the darkness. Your task is to explain the rise and fall of highway robbery and explain the factors behind the changes to this crime.

Activities

Work in groups. Your group will present your ideas to the rest of your class.

1 Sort the reasons shown around Source 1 below into:
   - reasons why highway robbery **increased**
   - reasons why highway robbery **declined**.

2 Order your reasons. Which was the most important reason why highway robbery
   a) increased
   b) declined?

3 You met the factors influencing crime earlier in your course (see page 7). Can you link them to the reasons why the crime of highway robbery rose or declined? Explain your ideas to your group – you have one minute to do this.

Source 1

There were many lonely areas outside towns for travellers to pass through.

Highwaymen could hide and sell their loot in taverns and inns.

Horses became cheaper to buy.

Guns were easier to obtain and use.

As the population expanded, open land was built on around towns.

Mounted patrols were set up around London.

Travellers no longer carried large sums of money – instead they used the new banks.

High rewards encouraged people to give information.

Some ex-soldiers became highwaymen as they couldn't find other jobs.

Roads improved and the traffic increased – there was less time between coaches.

▲ *A Highwayman hiding his loot in an Inn*, William Hogarth, 1747.

JPs refused to licence inns and taverns that aided highwaymen.

There was no police force and local constables did not try to track criminals.

Stagecoaches with guards were introduced to carry groups together.

People travelled alone in their own coaches.

How do attitudes affect what is a crime?

Your investigation of highway robbery has shown you that as well as understanding what a particular crime involved, you can also explain the factors underlying the crime and the changes that occurred. On pages 34–41 you will look at four crimes and for each one you should be able to:

- explain the key features of each crime – what it was and how it was punished
- explain the attitudes of criminals and law makers to the crime
- explain the factors behind the crime.

Activity 1: key features

Use the table below to list the key features of each crime and the punishments used to deal with it. Did the punishments change over time?

Crime	Description/dates	Punishments	Change
1 Treason			
2 Heresy			
3 Being a vagabond			
4 Poaching	Stealing wild animals from rich people's land	Execution	Punishment got harsher
5 Smuggling			

Activity 2: attitudes

Here you will evaluate the attitudes of law makers and ordinary people, using a new table for each crime like the one below. For each crime:

1 Decide the attitude of the law makers and ordinary people.   **2** Gather evidence to support your decision.

Poaching

	Serious crime	Minor crime	Not a crime	Evidence
Law makers' attitude	✓			death penalty
Ordinary people's attitude				

Activity 3: factors

Now you need to think about the underlying factors influencing these crimes and people's attitudes towards them. Look again at the factors wheel on page 7. For each crime list the factors under the following headings:

Crime	Factors that caused crime	Factors that affected attitudes	
		of law makers	of ordinary people
Treason	Religion – making disagreeing with the Protestant beliefs illegal.		
Poaching			Poverty meant that ordinary people believed poaching was necessary to survive.

Are any factors common across **all** crimes?

3.2 Why was religious opposition seen as a crime?

In 1534 Henry VIII changed England's religion. He left the Roman Catholic Church and set up the Protestant Church of England. These changes had a huge effect on people's lives, as you can see from Source 1. For the next few centuries arguments about religion took a central role in the way the country was run, and different religious views could be punishable by death!

The crimes people were punished for were:

Treason – disloyalty to the monarch or country. This was the crime when England was a Protestant country because the monarch was also the head of the Church of England. Punishment: execution.

Heresy – having beliefs that contradict Roman Catholic teachings. This was the crime when England was a Catholic country. Punishment: being burnt alive.

Activity

Complete your revision charts on these crimes: Treason and Heresy (see page 33).

Source 1

Services changed from Latin to English. Bibles in English were put in churches to encourage people to read and think for themselves.

Henry VIII's changes to religion

The appearance of churches changed – wall paintings were covered up, statues of saints removed and altars replaced with simple tables.

Monasteries were closed. They had not only provided a home and occupation for the monks and nuns, but had also given work to ordinary people and provided help to the poor.

Many saints' days and other festivals were banned – depriving people of age-old ceremonies which had been good excuses for drinking and having fun.

Priests were allowed to marry.

▲ Henry VIII made huge changes to religious life in England, and opposition to the ruling religion was definitely seen as a crime.

The Pilgrimage of Grace, 1536

Who – 30,000 ordinary people, led by a lawyer called Robert Aske.

Where – Northern parts of England, especially Yorkshire and Lincolnshire.

Why – They wanted to make England a Roman Catholic country again, to re-open monasteries and dismiss the King's advisors. Food prices were also high.

What – They marched through the north and took control of York, Hull and Pontefract. They were armed and wanted to talk to the King's advisors.

Punishment – 200 protestors were executed for their crime of treason during this protest. Robert Aske was hung, drawn and quartered in York, and his body parts hung in chains from York Castle.

Source 2

Henry VIII, 1537, explaining how the leaders of the Pilgrimage of Grace should be punished.

Cause such dreadful executions… hanging them on trees, quartering them, and setting the quarters in every town, as shall be a fearful warning.

Treason

Protestants, 1553–58

Who – Protestants who kept their faith when Mary turned England into a Catholic country again.

Where – All across England. Executions often took place where the people lived.

Why – People did not want to change their religious beliefs. However, the Queen saw heresy as a very serious crime. Protestants were also burnt alive in other European countries at this time.

What – The Protestants openly showed their beliefs and were tried according to the laws of heresy.

Punishment – Over 200 Protestants were estimated to have been executed for the crime of heresy during the reign of Queen Mary I. Archbishop Cranmer was kept in jail for two years before he was burnt alive in 1556.

Source 3

▲ Archbishop Cranmer being burnt at the stake, 1556, from a Protestant book made after Mary's reign ended.

Gunpowder plot, 1603

Who – A small group of rich Catholics. They invited Guy Fawkes, an ex-soldier, to join the plot as weapons specialist.

Where – Across England, but focused on killing the King in London.

Why – In 1603 King James declared his 'detestation' of Catholics and began to pass more laws against them. This group decided to act to remove him. Mistrust of Catholics had led James I's predecessor Elizabeth I to pass a law against 'wicked and seditious persons' calling themselves Catholics who were 'traitorous subjects' planning 'daily' plots, 'sedition and rebellion'! Prior to this law Elizabeth had tried to allow Catholics to live peacefully in her Protestant country.

What – The plotters hid gunpowder in cellars beneath Parliament and intended to blow up King James when he opened Parliament in November 1603. One plotter, Thomas Wintour, said the murder of the King would breed confusion which they could use to make England Catholic again.

Punishment – The plotters were rounded up and executed: dragged through crowds to the scaffold; hanged but not quite killed; taken down while alive; castrated, disembowelled and cut into quarters. The body parts were sent around the country as a warning. Guy Fawkes was tortured before he confessed. Ordinary Catholics had to pay a fine to be allowed to keep their beliefs.

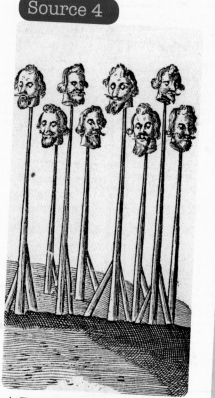

Source 4

▲ The plotters' heads placed on spikes. Cheap prints like this sold well.

3.3 Why was being homeless a crime in the 1500s?

Vagabond was a term used to describe the homeless in Tudor and Stuart England. Being a vagabond was a crime. On these pages you will continue your investigation into crimes, punishments and attitudes to crimes. Look at the information carefully – there is no simple explanation!

Activity

Add this crime – being a vagabond – to your revision chart (see page 33). Focus on the punishments, and the attitudes of ordinary people and law makers.

In 1575 Agnes Wort was whipped and her right ear was burnt because she was trying to find work.

The number of vagabonds increased periodically:
- after wars
- after bad harvests
- during trade slumps.

People believed harsh punishment would work as a deterrent against crime.

Source 1

◀ Books were becoming more popular and some of these had warnings about vagabonds. One book from 1567 by Thomas Harman described 23 different types of dangerous vagabond!

In 1528 many weavers lost their jobs when the cloth trade with the Netherlands was disrupted.

Religious ideas influenced laws – idleness was considered a sin and should be punished.

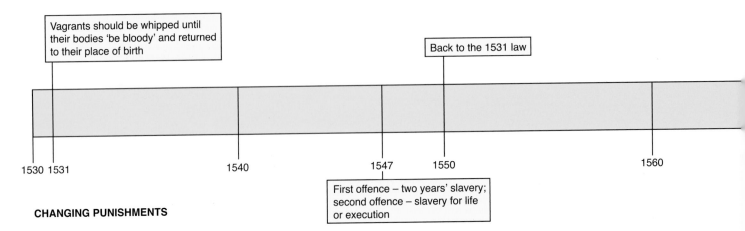

Vagrants should be whipped until their bodies 'be bloody' and returned to their place of birth

Back to the 1531 law

1530 1531   1540   1547   1550   1560

First offence – two years' slavery; second offence – slavery for life or execution

CHANGING PUNISHMENTS

36

The 1570s saw some particularly bad harvests.

Wages were very low in the late 1590s.

Local communities paid for the poor people in their area. The poor rates paid by communities increased as the number of poor people increased.

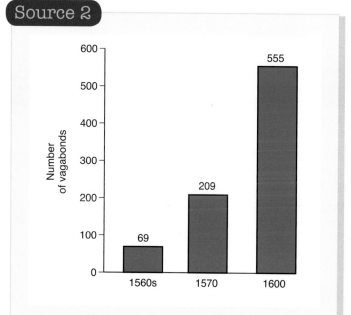

Source 2

▲ Graph showing the numbers of vagabonds in London's Bridewell Gaol each year. The number of vagabonds in London increased a lot and London was where laws were made.

Source 3

From a letter about increasing crime in Somerset written by Edward Hext, a magistrate.

I may justly say that the infinite numbers of idle, wandering people and robbers of the land are the chief cause of the problem because they labour not.

One religious pamphlet from 1579 said vagabonds should be punished because:
1 They spend their time in idleness when they might be working.
2 They waste their possessions and money in drinking.
3 They complain about other people's money when they have none themselves.
4 They do not go to church enough to learn their duties better.

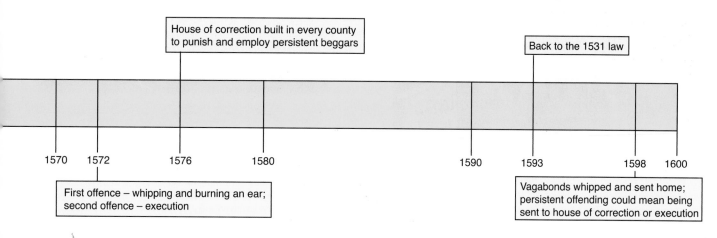

House of correction built in every county to punish and employ persistent beggars

Back to the 1531 law

1570   1572   1576   1580   1590   1593   1598   1600

First offence – whipping and burning an ear; second offence – execution

Vagabonds whipped and sent home; persistent offending could mean being sent to house of correction or execution

3.4 Why could eating meat lead to crime?

Poaching had been a crime since the Norman Forest laws were passed in 1080. In the later middle ages the punishments were reduced – but by the 18th century, punishments became harsher again. The Waltham Black Act of 1723 made the attitude of lawmakers very clear! But what did ordinary people think about this 'crime'?

All the quotations are from a book by the historian D. Hay, who researched poaching in Cannock Chase, England.

> For the men ... poaching was a 'custom of the manors' that they and their fathers had followed long before the Pagets [the rich landowners] acquired the land in the 16th century. It meant sport, money and a bit of meat.

> The great majority of middling men in rural England considered that the game laws were a great injustice. Middling men were convinced that a law banning anyone but major landowners from hunting was an oppression, and doubtless this view was held by the mass of labourers and cottagers.

Stages of poaching

1 The poacher or poaching gangs prepared for the night's hunting.
2 Animals were caught.
3 Some meat was eaten at home.
4 Other meat was taken to inns and sold on.

5 Coaches took the meat to towns and cities where it was sold to customers.

Activities

1 Find out the details of the crime; how it was punished; what attitudes people had to the crime – add your findings to your revision chart (see page 33).
2 Compare with modern poaching – what changes and continuity can you see?

WANTED...

... for POACHING

What was the crime?

What was the punishment?

Only those with land worth more than £100 were allowed to hunt at all – and they could hunt anywhere! £100 was more than many doctors earned in a whole year, and would be 10 years' wages for a labourer.

The big landowners controlled Parliament and the laws it made.

" For some villagers ... rather than being a supplement to an ill-paid or irregular job, poaching was the trade itself. "

" Any country inn-keeper could supply almost any quantity of game [bought from the poachers] and stage-waggoners on the great roads acted as agents for London buyers. "

Possessing dogs or snares that could be used for poaching was punished by a £5 fine or three months in prison.

" The poachers sometimes resorted to ... violence. "

" All the evidence suggests that this small community of labourers, colliers and farmers was united solidly in defence of poaching. "

1723 Waltham Black Act – poaching deer, rabbits or hare was punishable by death. Going out at night with a blackened face for camouflage was enough to have you executed on the assumption of poaching!

Laws still used today:
1828 Night Poaching Act – illegal to be on any land at night with the intention of poaching.
1862 Poaching Prevention Act – any person or suspicious vehicle can be stopped and searched.

" Farmers and tradesmen made up the juries at courts. As one steward complained 'there is no answering for a common jury as they have in general a strong bias in favour of poachers'. "

Modern poaching

- Game animals are still taken from land and estates.
- Mixture of individual poachers and professional gangs.
- Endangered animals are poached and their parts smuggled into the UK.
- In 2008 two poachers were fined £7,000 for stealing bluebell bulbs.

3.5 Why could drinking tea lead to crime?

Drinking tea has been a national obsession in Britain for hundreds of years – but during the 18th century it led to a crime that was punishable by death. Thousands of people regularly broke the law just to get a cup of their favourite drink. Can you think of any reason why this would have been the case? Investigate the information and see if you can find out why – and suggest an effective way to solve this crime.

John Taylor, keeper of Newgate Gaol, 1747: The common people of England fancy there is nothing in the crime of smuggling ... they feel they have a right to shun paying any duty [tax] on their goods.

Robert Walpole, who later became Prime Minister, used government ships to smuggle wine in the 1700s.

The tax on tea reached 119 per cent by the mid 18th century!

A letter from the Duke of Richmond to Sir Cecil Bishop, 1749: 'I have often heard you say and with great truth, that the common people of this country have no notion that smuggling is a crime. What then can the government do to show them their error but to punish the guilty?'

Activities

1 Find out the details of the crime; how it was punished; what attitudes people had to the crime – add your findings to your revision chart (see page 33).

2 Compare with modern smuggling – what changes and continuity can you see?

3 How would you have solved the crime if **you** were a law maker?

Stages of smuggling

1 A ship moored off shore with smuggled goods brought over from Europe.
2 Teams of smugglers brought the goods to shore as night fell.
3 The goods were taken inland and carried to towns.
4 The smugglers could be in London by 2am and sell well over 1,000 pounds of tea by 6am to the duffers – illegal tea dealers.
5 The duffers sold the tea on to hawkers who carried it around town and sold it to their customers.

WANTED...

... for SMUGGLING

What was the crime?

What was the punishment?

Attitude of the lawmaker

Smuggling levels varied with the tax on tea. Tea duty was raised in 1711 and in the 1750s to help raise funds for wars – as a result, smuggling levels increased. Then, in 1784, Pitt the Younger reduced the tea duty from 119% to 12.5% and smuggling tea was no longer profitable!

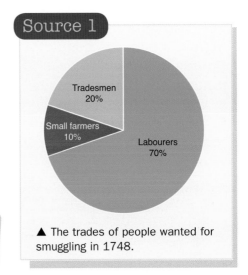

▲ The trades of people wanted for smuggling in 1748.

Anyone who helped to bring goods from the ship to the shore could earn twice a labourer's daily wage.

The Gentleman's magazine, 1747: 'About 24 smugglers well-armed and laden with smuggled goods rode through Rye, Sussex and stopping at the Red Lion to refresh, fired several times to intimidate the inhabitants.'

Customs officers had large areas to patrol and often worked alone against large gangs.

In Suffolk the army was used in the 1780s to stop smuggling; many smugglers turned to other crimes like highway robbery to earn the same amount of money.

A smuggler could earn six or seven times a farm labourer's daily wage in just one night.

Three-quarters of all tea in the country was estimated to be smuggled tea.

Samuel Wilson, a Sussex grocer who had received smuggled tea, gave evidence to Parliament in the 1740s: '... the people on the coasts are better friends to smugglers than they are to Custom House Officers'.

Batsmen were armed smugglers whose job was to protect the cargo as it was landed.

Modern smuggling

- Alcohol and tobacco are smuggled by individuals to avoid tax.
- Planes, boats, trucks and people are used by gangs to smuggle illegal drugs and alcohol.
- People are smuggled to work as prostitutes or illegal labourers.
- Drug packages are sometimes swallowed by 'mules'.
- Punishments vary depending on what has been smuggled – from fines to prison.

What attitudes do people today have to the different aspects of modern smuggling?

◄ A taped-up packet stuffed with drugs. Up to 30 packets can be swallowed by 'mules' (people paid to smuggle them) and collected on arrival when they have gone through the body.

3.6 Did crime change in the 19th century?

The 19th century was a time of great change: the population rapidly increased to over 40 million; the majority moved to towns and cities; technology and working conditions altered. Look back to the Criminal Moments in Time (pages 12–17), to see what other changes to society you can see. But did crime, and the way people explained crime, change greatly too?

Activities

1 Work in pairs. Look at the graph in Source 1 and summarise the patterns in the crime rate. What information on pages 42–43 helps you to explain the changes? Take turns to explain it to each other. You should agree on an answer before you write it down.

2 Look at the sources from the time about how people explained the crime rate then. Sort it into the following categories:
   • Blame the criminals for being naturally bad
   • Blame society for making people into criminals
   • Blame other factors influencing the criminals.

3 Look again at the factors on page 7. Which ones affected the 1800s?

The end of the French Wars in 1815 led to increased unemployment and poverty which led to increased crime and protests about food prices.

The government published official crime statistics annually after 1810.

New laws affected figures: between 1870 and 1890 half a million parents were prosecuted for not sending their children to school.

Source 1

▲ A graph showing trends in crime, 1750–1900.

There was widespread fear of crime, especially amongst the upper and middle classes.

Newspapers concentrated on violent crimes.

Only ten per cent of crimes involved violence.

Until the 1840s there was a fear that revolution would spread from France to England and Wales.

New technology saw many people lose their jobs.

Some crimes were cracked down on to set an example.

Seventy-five per cent of criminals were young men.

Seventy per cent of crime was minor thefts.

Source 2

The *Morning Star*, a London newspaper, 18 January 1861.

Owing to the continuance of the frost and all outdoor labour being stopped, the distress and suffering amongst the labouring classes are truly horrible. On Tuesday night an attack was made on a large number of bakers' shops. On Wednesday night an attack was made on many of the bakers' shops and eating houses. A great many thieves mingled with the mob and many serious acts of violence were committed.

Source 3

Edwin Chadwick, reporting in a Royal Commission in 1839.

We have investigated the origin of the great mass of crime and we find one common cause – namely the temptations of profit from a career of theft as compared with the profits of honest men and even well-paid work. The idea that any considerable number of crimes are caused by poverty we find disproved at every step.

Source 4

The Times newspaper in 1884 said that an 18-year-old who shot a policeman had 'been corrupted by reading trashy literature'.

Source 5

The Times newspaper, 2 December 1843, reporting on 'criminal' protestors in Wales. *The Times* was a London newspaper associated with the rich and middle classes.

The main cause of the disturbances is the poverty of the people ... The condition of the farm labourers is terrible. They live entirely on potatoes, and seldom have enough of them. They have one meal a day. They live in mud cottages with only one room.

Source 6

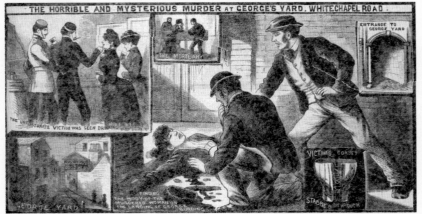

▲ A tabloid newspaper from 1888, full of gruesome stories about crime. Many people said these newspapers and 'penny dreadful' novels were turning the poor into worse criminals by glamorising law-breakers!

Source 7

J W Horsley, 1898. Horsley was an anti-alcohol campaigner and worked as chaplain at Clerkenwell Prison in London.

Half the causes of common assault and three-quarters of assaults on the police were committed by drunken persons. Cruelty to animals and children – of these, half might fairly be considered caused by drink. Then there are the cases which are indirectly caused by drink, for example, thefts by or from drunken persons. The conclusion that drink causes half of all crime directly and one-quarter indirectly is a modest estimate.

Source 8

Judge M Hill gave evidence to Parliament about crime in 1852.

A century and a half ago there was scarcely a town where a poor person was not known to the majority of the townspeople. In small towns there must be a sort of natural police ... But in a large town he lives in absolute obscurity which to a certain extent gives safety against being punished.

Source 9

◄ A prisoner in Bedford Gaol. There was a new theory that criminal characteristics were inherited, and that this could be identified by the shape of the head and animal-like expressions. The theory was influenced by Darwin's ideas about evolution. By 1870 prisoners had their photographs taken, and details of their background and crimes were recorded to help identify this criminal class.

3.7 How did crime change in the 20th century?

You have investigated the patterns of crime in the 19th century. But what has changed in the last 100 years or so?

Activities

On page 6 you considered whether or not modern crimes were new, or were just new versions of old crimes. There were certainly lots of new laws passed in the 20th century. In this task you should give some specific details about these laws and refer to the attitudes that made them crimes.

1 Work in groups. Each group should take one of the crime files on these pages. Create a presentation showing the following key points:
   • What the crime is
   • What the punishment is
   • When the law came into effect
   • Why it became a crime (look at the factor wheel on page 7)
   • If it is a new crime or a version of an old crime – back this up with evidence!
2 Research newspaper articles about this crime. What attitudes do the articles show? How does this influence fear of this crime?
3 Suggest solutions and the punishment you would like to see for this crime.

Source 1

England and Wales	22.7
Scotland	15.5
Average in Europe	9.5

▲ Number of cars stolen per 100,000 of population (1996).

File 1: Car crime

In 1900 the motor car had only just been invented. Now car crime is one of the biggest categories of crime – ranging from drunk driving to car theft. In 1996 there were almost 1.3 million crimes involving cars; nearly half a million cars were stolen! However, since then, improved car security has led to a halving of car theft.

A blood alcohol limit tested by a breathalyser came into law in 1967. The drink driving penalties have since increased: in 2004 the maximum sentence for causing death by drunk driving was raised to 14 years. New technology also means that speed cameras can record offences without a person needing to be present.

File 2: Tax evasion

People try to avoid tax in two main ways: smuggling taxed goods like tobacco and alcohol; paying accountants to ensure they pay the minimum possible tax. If you are caught with these smuggled goods you can be fined or even sent to jail. Accountants help ensure that tax evasion is kept within the law; many high earning celebrities officially live in other countries to avoid paying tax. The government is constantly trying to find ways to ensure that all tax is collected and there is a tax evasion hotline phone number for people to give information about this crime.

File 3: Computer crime

As technology has changed, computers have given criminals new opportunities for crime. Internet credit card crime was estimated to cost the taxpayer over £212 million in 2006. Phishing scams try to trick people into giving criminals key information like passwords. In 2007 the law was changed to make banks responsible for investigating fraud. In 2008 a special police unit was set up to stop this crime. Computers are also used by paedophiles to share obscene images and to 'groom' their victims in chatrooms.

File 4: Discrimination

The Sex Discrimination Act of 1975 made it illegal to discriminate against women. Despite this, in 2009 the Office for National Statistics showed that women earn 12% less than men and the *Observer* newspaper reported that 'traditional chauvinism [male sexist attitudes to women] is the real obstacle to women' in the work place (*Observer* 19 April 2009).

In 1995 a new law extended similar rights to people with disabilities.

File 5: Racist crime

The first Race Relations Act came into force in 1965, making it illegal to discriminate in public places like cinemas, buses and hotels. The Race Relations Act 1976 made workplace discrimination illegal. 2006 saw a new Religious and Racial Hatred law. In 2007, The Metropolitan Police recorded 8,818 racist incidents in London – they are part of the 'hate crime' figures. A study in 1997 showed that 70% of racist incidents involved more than verbal abuse.

Source 2

Trevor Phillips, 2005.

The fact that we have strong anti-discrimination laws has led to the near disappearance of commonplace practices which disfigured our society. That does not mean they don't ever happen but today they are the exception rather than the rule.

File 6: Hooliganism

Poor behaviour by football fans was a particular concern of law makers in the late twentieth century. In 2000 banning orders were introduced, which means violent hooligans and racists can be banned from football grounds for between 2 and 10 years. In the 2007/08 season 1,048 of these orders were made; the club with the worst record was Manchester United, with 248 fans arrested at games. A special police unit was set up to deal with football crime in 1998; this was developed into the UK Football Policing Unit in 2005.

File 7: Sexual offences

Concern over sex offences continues to grow. The police and courts were given new guidelines for treating rape cases, and punishments have changed. At times there has been a great deal of sensational media coverage about these cases, leading to a moral panic and pressure for new laws. In 1997 the Sex Offenders Act was introduced, which means that anyone cautioned or convicted for a sexual offence must be placed on the Sex Offenders Register, which is monitored by the police. In 2006 there were 29,000 people on the register. If you are jailed for more than 30 months for a sexual offence you are not allowed off the register.

Crime levels increased in the early 1990s but have now returned to roughly the same levels as 1981. There is no easy explanation for this – some ideas include:

- Stolen goods are worth less.
- The way crimes are recorded have changed.
- More criminals are sent to jail than before.
- Better security on cars.
- New ideas about punishment have been tried.

Look back to the factor wheel on page 7. What factors do you think are at work here?

Source 3

▲ The wreckage of a bus bombed by a group linked to Al Qaeda in London in July 2005.

File 8: Terrorism

Britain lived with the threat of terrorism for much of the 20th century – as long ago as the 1930s British troops in Palestine were attacked. However, from the 1960s the threat was more common, for example from the IRA trying to end British rule in Northern Ireland, or the Unionist groups opposing them. More recently the threat has come from other groups linked to Al Qaeda. In July 2005 four bombs were set off in London on the Tube and on a bus. Many new laws were passed to deal with the threat of terrorism. The 2006 Terrorism Act means that anyone preparing for a terrorist act can be imprisoned for life, and anyone convicted of encouraging terrorism can be jailed for 7 years.

Meet the Examiner: Analysing factors

Some questions in the exam ask you to demonstrate your knowledge of something and to analyse the factors involved. This type of question usually carries a lot of marks.

The examiners also like to give you some information to help you to remember. Try to plan your own answer **before** you look at this information. Show your own knowledge; don't just rely on this.

You have already been introduced to the key factors which help to explain the attitudes to a particular crime or punishment (see page 7). These pages will help you to use them to tackle this sort of 'analysing factors' question.

Look at the question below. The question has been decoded for you.

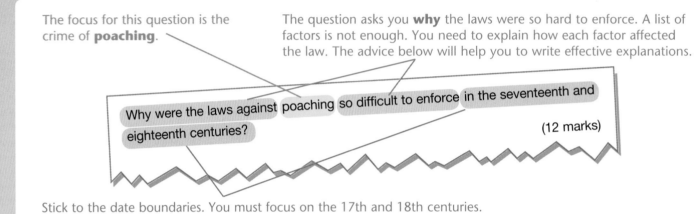

The focus for this question is the crime of **poaching**.

The question asks you **why** the laws were so hard to enforce. A list of factors is not enough. You need to explain how each factor affected the law. The advice below will help you to write effective explanations.

Why were the laws against poaching so difficult to enforce in the seventeenth and eighteenth centuries?

(12 marks)

Stick to the date boundaries. You must focus on the 17th and 18th centuries. Mentioning Medieval or modern poaching will not get you any marks.

How to write effective explanations

Step 1: Identify the range of factors

List all the factors that help to explain why laws against poaching were hard to enforce. Use the concept map technique on pages 98–99 to help you. Before the exam try this technique also on laws to do with smuggling or why vagabonds were punished the way they were.

Step 2: Select two or three factors to write about

Do not try to cover everything. Remember that in an exam you have only about 15 minutes to answer this type of question. Choose the two or three main factors and answer them in detail.

Step 3: Use connectives to tie in your knowledge to the question

Don't just say a factor was important.
a) Show off your knowledge and **prove it** with evidence! Use your own evidence, not just the example the exam question may give you.

For example ...

b) Explain how each factor was a problem for this law. Use connectives such as:

This meant that ... This resulted in ...

Activity

Look at the answer opposite. The student has used connectives to link one factor to difficulties in enforcing the law. That's one paragraph done. Now have a go at producing another paragraph yourself. Focus on a different factor. You can use the sentence starters and connectives provided in Step 3 **or** you can use your own.

One reason why poaching laws were hard to enforce was to do with the roles of government and law makers.

The student identifies a factor – roles of government.

The law makers kept making the laws harsher and trying as hard as possible to keep the profit from all the animals on their land, even the wild ones. It made people see the law as harsh and unfair, and kept the price of meat higher than many could afford.

The student gives further details about this factor.

For example you had to own land worth £100 before you could hunt. Furthermore the Waltham Black Act of 1723 meant that you could be executed for going out at night with camouflage on. You did not even have to actually catch an animal to be hanged!

The student gives a precise example to support his argument.

This meant the majority of the population were not allowed to hunt legally. Even doctors did not earn this much in a year and would become criminals if they did any hunting at all. It also meant that juries might not find someone guilty if they thought the punishment was unfair – and most of the people who sat on juries would not have been able to hunt either.

The student clearly ties this factor to the question.

Another important factor was the belief that ordinary people had a right to hunt. They felt it had always been that way, and new laws would not stop them. For example ... (look for a relevant 'quotation' here) This meant that ...

Step 4: Structure your conclusion so that it clearly analyses the factors

Start by showing that a range of factors played a role.

As has been shown these laws were hard to introduce because of the attitudes towards them and the impact on the majority of the country.

Make it clear which factor you think played the most important role.

The main reason was the way the harsh government laws criminalised most of the country, including the people who sat on juries.

Support your argument with the key reason why you have come to this overall judgement.

Overall people might have felt they had a right to hunt, but the fact that juries and respectable people did not support the laws meant that they would always be difficult to carry out.

Your conclusion is very important. It should be short and focus on the question. It is not a detailed summary of everything you have written.

Section 4: Was there a revolution in punishment?

In this section you will look at how, and why, punishments changed in the 18th and 19th centuries. Just as there were revolutionary changes in industry, agriculture and even politics during this time, some historians would argue that there was a revolution in punishment. Like many revolutions, it was not a straightforward process. At times the changes may seem harsh – our modern thinking is not the same as that of the past. However, it is more important for us to understand a) what happened and b) the attitudes behind the changes.

Let us start with a game, a game with a purpose. By playing it you can start to generate some ideas about punishments in the 1700s. Your studies will then add depth to your ideas. Your objective is to survive and escape being hanged. The people you will be playing were real – these are their stories and it was not a game to them.

Activities

When you have finished playing, write your answers to these questions:

1. What sort of crimes led to people being hanged in the 1700s?
2. Why did some people escape being hanged? Why didn't other people escape?
3. Were the laws fair in the 1700s?

How to play:

1. Get into groups of three. You will each need a counter to move around the board.
2. Each choose a character. Put your counter on their starting square. Note down your name, age and crime.
3. Take turns to move, following the instructions in each square.
4. When your fate has been decided note down a) how you were punished and b) why you were punished. Repeat the game using the other three characters.

Characters

Roderick Audrey, aged 16. Start at square 18.

Ann Collins, aged 20. Start at square 15.

Doctor Dodd, one of the King's chaplains. Start at square 10.

William York, aged 10. Start at square 13.

Elizabeth Hardy, aged 19. Start at square 2.

Charles Macklin, a famous actor. Start at square 7.

Who will hang?

1	2	3	4
You are convicted of manslaughter. You are set free after being branded on the hand.	You are accused of stealing goods worth 13 shillings and sixpence. Go to square 19.	You are sentenced to hang and the execution is carried out.	Your wealthy and well-known friends tell the court that you have a good character and collect signatures on a petition to save your life. Go to square 20.
5	**6**	**7**	**8**
The jury hears that you trained birds to fly through open windows so that if you were caught inside a house, you could claim you were only trying to get your bird back. Go to square 9.	You are desperate to speak up for yourself in court. To give yourself courage you have a drink of gin. Go to square 12.	You are accused of killing another actor in an argument. Go to square 16.	The court recommends that you should hang, but the judge discusses your case with other judges because of your age. Go to square 21.
9	**10**	**11**	**12**
You do not know any respectable people who could speak to the court on your behalf. Go to square 3.	You are accused of forgery and of obtaining £4,300 under false pretences. Go to square 4.	You are sentenced to death. However, there has not been very much crime recently and the court is sorry for you. Go to square 24.	You drank too much. The judge thinks that you are rude when you try to defend yourself and that you do not respect him or his court. Go to square 3.
13	**14**	**15**	**16**
You are accused of murdering a five-year-old girl. Go to square 23.	After nine years you are reprieved from hanging when you agree to join the navy and leave the country.	You are accused of stealing goods worth a pound but you are innocent. Go to square 6.	Your wealthy and well-known friends tell the court that you have a good character. Go to square 22.
17	**18**	**19**	**20**
The King and government believe that forgery is a most serious crime. Go to square 3.	You are accused of stealing from houses. Go to square 5.	You tell the jury that your husband deserted you, leaving you alone and without work in London. Go to square 11.	The jury finds you guilty, but recommends that you be reprieved from hanging. Go to square 17.
21	**22**	**23**	**24**
The judge decides that you are to be imprisoned until a final decision is made. You could still be sentenced to hang. Go to square 14.	Your acting skills come in useful. You show great respect for the judge and say how sorry you are for the accident. Go to square 1.	The jury hear that you planned the crime carefully and carried it out in cold blood. Go to square 8.	You are reprieved from hanging and sentenced to transportation to America.

4.1 What was the Bloody Code?

Today if you stole a silk handkerchief what would your punishment be? Would you be more likely to be warned, fined or executed? Execution may seem like a ridiculous punishment for a relatively minor crime, but in the 18th century it was regularly handed down. Source 1 shows you how many **capital crimes** there actually were. In 1723 alone, 50 new crimes were added by the Waltham Black Act. Judges would put black caps on top of their ceremonial wigs before declaring that the sentence would be death. The laws were so harsh that historians have given them the nickname of the Bloody Code.

Source 1

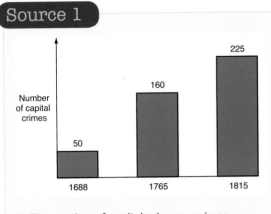

▲ The number of capital crimes – crimes carrying the death penalty.

Activities

1 Look at the list of capital crimes below. Sort them into the following categories:
   - minor property crime
   - serious property crime
   - violent crime.

2 Why do you think so many more minor crimes became punishable by death in 1723?

3 What does it tell us about the attitude of law makers?

4 Why do you think the legal system got the nickname of the Bloody Code?

5 What can you learn from Source 2 about the artist's attitude to the Bloody Code and the death penalty?

6 Why do you think executions were held in public? Think back to what you learned in the Big Story at the start of your course.

Some capital crimes

Stealing horses

Destroying turnpike roads

Cutting down wood from growing trees

Pick-pocketing goods worth more than one shilling

Arson

Shoplifting goods worth more than five shillings

Destroying fish ponds

Treason

Smuggling

Sending threatening letters

Vandalising Westminster Bridge

Begging if you are a soldier or sailor

FORGERY

Stealing from a rabbit warren

Breaking tools used to make wool

BEING OUT AT NIGHT WITH A CAMOUFLAGED FACE

Murder

Source 2

▲ This cartoon from 1831 by William Heath has an ironic title: Merry England.

Alternative punishments to execution

Judges could use a range of other punishments too. Some were old punishments and some were new – a mixture of **change** and **continuity**.

The pillory was used to punish cheating at cards, selling underweight or rotten goods and sometimes persistent swearing. Some criminals sentenced to the pillory did not suffer at all. A man who was pilloried for refusing to pay the tax on soap had an hour of being cheered by the crowd! However the pillory could become a death sentence. Two men who had won £4,000 playing with loaded dice were pelted with stones. Criminals convicted of sexual crimes, particularly involving children, were likely to be attacked and sometimes killed in the pillory.

A

The stocks were used mainly for those who could not afford to pay fines, often imposed for drunkenness.

B

The ducking stool was used to punish women who had been convicted of being scolds, which meant swearing or arguing in public, trouble-making or arguing with their husbands and not obeying them as wives were supposed to.

C

Carting meant being paraded around the streets in a cart and was used to punish adultery or running a brothel.

D

Many minor offences such as swearing, gambling, drunkenness and failing to attend church occasionally were punished by **fines**.

E

Whipping usually took place on market day so it could be as public as possible. Whipping was ordered for a wide variety of offences: vagrancy; the theft of goods worth less than a shilling; drunkeness; and regular refusal to attend church. On one occasion two men were whipped in London, one for stealing a radish, the other for child abuse. By the 1700s whipping was less common because transportation was used regularly as a punishment.

F

Many towns built a **House of Correction** in the late 1500s, to punish and reform offenders. The first of these was the Bridewell Palace in London and so all came to be known as Bridewells. Vagrants, unmarried mothers and runaway apprentices were sent to the Bridewell where they were whipped and set to hard work. They were also used as an extra punishment when other punishments or warnings had not worked. The authorities believed that crimes were usually a result of not working hard enough.

G

The greatest change in punishments was **transportation**. Criminals were sent to the American colonies from the 1660s but the numbers became much more frequent after the Transportation Act of 1718. Between 1718 and 1769, 70 per cent of the criminals convicted at the Old Bailey in London were transported. In all 36,000 people were transported. It became a routine sentence – of 7 years, 14 years or life depending on the crime. Charles Scoldwell was transported for 7 years for stealing two ducks. Murderers who escaped the noose went for life. Once in America the punishment was meant to be harsh. Some suffered conditions close to slavery. However it was criticised in England by those who thought it a soft option.

H

4.2 Was the Bloody Code really so bloody?

As you have seen, the number of crimes punishable by death increased greatly in the 18th and early 19th century. You might therefore expect a similar increase in the number of people executed. But was this actually the case? For this enquiry you will need to look at the statistics as well as traditional evidence. Statistics are an interesting form of evidence, and can give a historian like you insights into the past.

Activities

Use the sources and information on pages 52–53 to investigate the hypothesis that 'The Bloody Code led to an increase in executions'.

1 Make a living graph like the one below. Start by drawing your own blank graph.

Information AGREES

If the information *agrees* with the hypothesis, place the sticky note above the line

Time

If the information *disagrees* with the hypothesis, place the sticky note below the line

Information DISAGREES

2 Start with Sources 1–3. Summarise each on its own sticky note. Include:
   a) when it is from
   b) where the evidence is from
   c) what it tells us about the Bloody Code.

3 Now do the same for the other bits of information.

4 Organise your notes in chronological order. Some information may not fit easily. Have reasons for the decisions you make.

5 What is the overall pattern that the information tells us – does it support or disagree with the hypothesis? Can you think of any reasons why?

Source 1

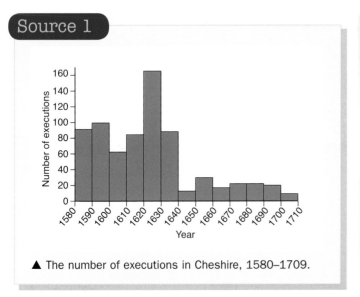

▲ The number of executions in Cheshire, 1580–1709.

Thirty per cent of accused people were pardoned in the 1700s. Juries thought punishments were too harsh.

At the start of the 1700s, 200 people a year were executed across the whole of England and Wales.

If you showed remorse for your crime you were likely to have your sentence reduced.

During wars criminals could join the navy or army instead of being executed.

Stop! Be careful, statistics can be dangerous! You can draw your own conclusions by looking at statistics, but you need to be aware of the limits of your data. For example, is the evidence from the whole of the country or just one county? If it is just one county, can you safely generalise about everywhere else? You should show the examiner you are aware of this.
Try saying 'The evidence from _____ suggests that ...'.

One girl turned up drunk to the court in London. Even though she was found innocent of her crime she was hanged for showing disrespect to the judge.

Source 2

A comparison of executions in Devon and London. The numbers are the average number of executions in each year in the decades listed.

	1600–1610	1700–1710
London	150	20
Devon	25	3

Source 3

▲ Number of criminals *sentenced* to death at The Old Bailey courthouse in London. Many of these had their sentence reduced. Some may have died in prison from disease before they could be executed – mortality rates were 30 per cent in gaols.

There were occasional peaks in hangings when law makers were worried about rising crime or protests and wanted to set an example.

In the 1700s over 100 women had their death sentences reduced at the Old Bailey because they were pregnant.

If you had rich or respectable friends who could stand up for your good character you were likely to avoid execution.

From 1700 to 1750, only 10 per cent of those sentenced to death in London were actually hanged.

In 1833 Lord Suffield pointed out that of 1,100 people sentenced to hang for housebreaking in the previous two years, only one person had actually been executed.

If you showed respect for the court you were likely to have your sentence reduced from death.

Charles Macklin, a famous actor, murdered another man in London – but his rich friends spoke in court and he was punished only by being branded on the hand.

Attitude of law makers

Some law makers would have argued that the information on these pages proved that the law was working – that it was flexible and acting as a deterrent. The clergyman Archdeacon William Paley shows us this attitude.

> The best way to frighten people away from crime is severe punishment. Therefore, as many crimes as possible should be punished with execution. We do not need to hang everyone convicted of these crimes, of course; just enough to keep people aware of the danger of committing crimes. The innocent may be hanged now and again but that is the price that must be paid for stopping crime. An innocent man who is hanged is dying for the good of his country.

In theory everyone convicted of a serious crime such as murder or theft of goods worth more than 1 shilling would be hanged. However only 25 per cent of those who were convicted were hanged. Many were saved because the jury decided that the stolen goods were worth less than 1 shilling or women were spared because they claimed to be pregnant. Many others escaped because they were able to read the 'neck verse' you read about on page 27. Although benefit of clergy no longer applied to murder, many people were convicted of manslaughter and so still claimed benefit of clergy. Those who were actually hanged were likely to be persistently dangerous and violent or regular thieves.

4.3 Why did the Bloody Code end?

You have already seen that the number of capital crimes continued to grow in the 1700s. But by the late 18th century ideas about punishment began to change, and by 1841 only three crimes were still punishable by death: murder, piracy and treason. The man responsible for changing the law was Sir Robert Peel, who was Home Secretary in the 1820s. You will learn more about him later in this book. But what new ideas led to this dramatic change, especially during a time of rising crime?

Activities

Your task is to investigate the information and persuade the Home Secretary, Sir Robert Peel, that the time has come to get rid of the Bloody Code.

1 Work in pairs and look at the information on pages 54–55. Then copy and complete the table below. Remember to write in full sentences.

2 Write a persuasive speech to give in Parliament – use the skills of persuasive writing you have learned in your English lessons to help you. You should think about:

- Paragraph order
- Rhetorical questions
- Repetition
- Vocabulary
- Connectives
- Fact/Opinion
- Appealing directly to the audience.

3 Practise giving your speech. You should think about your tone, volume, movement and eye contact. These will all help your persuasive writing be more effective.

Punishments don't fit the crime.

The Bloody Code laws aren't working.

Executions aren't deterring criminals.

	New ways of thinking	How convincing is it?	Information to support this	Why would this convince Peel to change the laws?
1	Punishments do not fit the crime			
2	Public executions are not a deterrent			
3	The laws aren't working – crime is still going up			
4	The laws aren't working – juries will not convict for minor crimes			
5	Other ideas			

4 Overall, which was the most important reason for ending the Bloody Code?

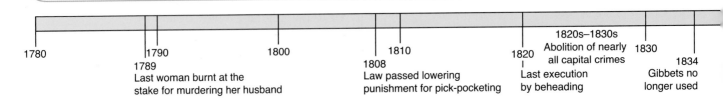

1780 1790 1800 1810 1820 1830

1789
Last woman burnt at the stake for murdering her husband

1808
Law passed lowering punishment for pick-pocketing

1820s–1830s
Abolition of nearly all capital crimes

1820
Last execution by beheading

1834
Gibbets no longer used

Public executions were no longer seen as a useful deterrent.

In 1783 London's magistrates said 'all the aims of public justice are defeated. All the terrors of death, the shame of punishment, are lost.'

Magistrate Henry Fielding, 1751.

Execution should in some way be private.

The government worried about keeping order at hangings and moved them next to gaols. Crowds at executions had grown larger, as newspapers publicised hangings, and there were often rowdy, drunken mobs. The possibility of escape or riot was another worry, especially if the prisoners were popular with the crowd or the crowd thought the punishment unfair.

Source 2

Ceasare Beaccaria's influential book was first published in English in 1767.

Current punishments do not fit the crime ... We need punishments that fit the crimes. Instead of relying on the death penalty, criminals should be imprisoned and do hard labour that is visible to the public.

Source 3

Bernard Mandeville, describing the spectacle of executions in London in 1725.

All the way, from Newgate to Tyburn, is one continued fair for rogues and whores of the meaner sort ... instead of giving warning, they are exemplary the wrong way, and encourage where they should deter.

Some factories closed for the day if there was an execution to watch!

The Enlightenment was a new way of thinking. Part of it was that punishments should match the crime; also it was thought that criminals could be reformed and made into useful members of society.

Source 4

The reforming MP William Meredith, 1770.

A man who has picked the pocket of a handkerchief worth thirteen pence is punished with the same severity as if he had murdered a whole family.

New punishments like transportation had already been tried. This had been very successful. Most of those transported had originally been sentenced to death, then had the punishment reduced. Transported prisoners had often become reformed characters.

In the 1700s only 40 per cent of those sentenced to death were actually hanged. By the 1800s this fell to 10 per cent.

Juries would often not convict people for minor crimes as they thought the punishment was unfair. This meant that the punishments were actually stopping the laws from working. The Bloody Code was not protecting the property of the rich and middle classes. Criminals might even be more likely to commit crime!

1840   1850   1860   1870

1841
Only murder, treason and
piracy punishable by death

1868
Last public
hanging

4.4 Why was transportation used as a punishment?

An alternative to hanging that was increasingly used in the 1700s was transportation – the removal of criminals to other countries owned by Britain. At first America was used, but after the 1770s when America became independent, Australia was the destination for thousands of criminals.

For this enquiry you will be trying to answer the question: Why was transportation used as a punishment?

In total, over 160,000 people were transported to Australia – for sentences ranging from seven years to life – as this graph shows:

Source 1

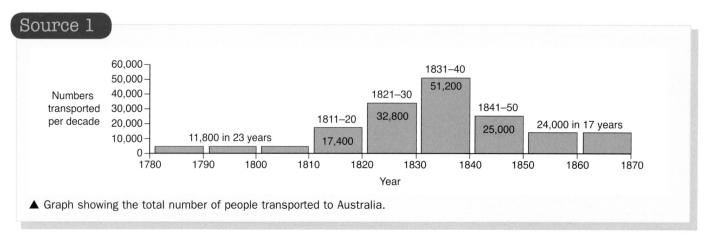

▲ Graph showing the total number of people transported to Australia.

One sort of criminal who often faced this punishment was the political protestor or rioter. After the French Revolution, and also the assassination of the British Prime Minister in 1812, the authorities were eager to clamp down on anyone involved in unrest, as the story of the Tolpuddle Martyrs in 1833 shows.

Tolpuddle Martyrs

- In 1833 George Loveless and five other farm workers in Tolpuddle, Dorset met in secret. They swore an oath to join a trade union. This was not illegal.
- However employers did not like the idea of unions and tried to break them up. They were also scared it would lead to a return of the Swing Riots of three years earlier.
- A local magistrate used a law meant only for the navy to arrest the six men and put them on trial.
- An unfair jury found them guilty and they were sentenced to seven years' transportation to Australia.
- They worked like other transported criminals did – hard labour in difficult conditions.
- There was a great campaign to have them released. One petition was signed by more than 250,000 people – in 1836 they were released and returned to England.

◀ A demonstration in London on 21 April 1834 in protest at the deportation of the Tolpuddle Martyrs

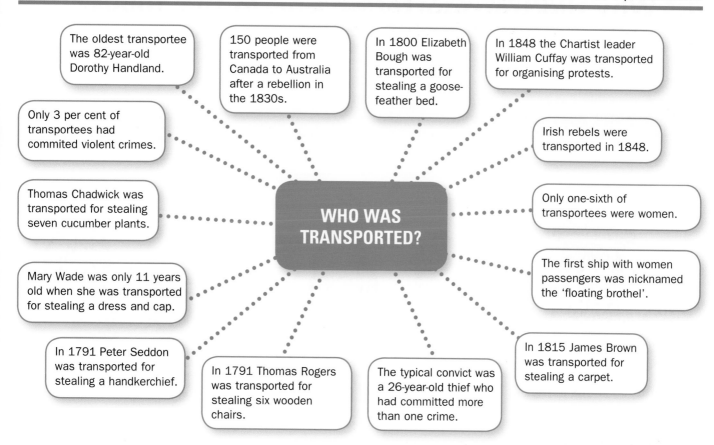

WHO WAS TRANSPORTED?

The oldest transportee was 82-year-old Dorothy Handland.

150 people were transported from Canada to Australia after a rebellion in the 1830s.

In 1800 Elizabeth Bough was transported for stealing a goose-feather bed.

In 1848 the Chartist leader William Cuffay was transported for organising protests.

Only 3 per cent of transportees had commited violent crimes.

Irish rebels were transported in 1848.

Thomas Chadwick was transported for stealing seven cucumber plants.

Only one-sixth of transportees were women.

Mary Wade was only 11 years old when she was transported for stealing a dress and cap.

The first ship with women passengers was nicknamed the 'floating brothel'.

In 1791 Peter Seddon was transported for stealing a handkerchief.

In 1791 Thomas Rogers was transported for stealing six wooden chairs.

The typical convict was a 26-year-old thief who had committed more than one crime.

In 1815 James Brown was transported for stealing a carpet.

Why?

So why was this punishment used? What made the law makers increasingly move from execution to transportation as a way of dealing with law-breakers?

Reasons for introducing transportation

a) Just like hanging, **transportation removed the criminals from Britain** and thereby reduced crime.

b) **Transportation would reform the criminals**: they would work and learn new, useful skills so they would be less likely to reoffend.

c) **It was an alternative to hanging.** Juries often found people innocent if they thought the punishment would be death. Prison was thought to be too expensive at the time. Transportation was seen as 'the middle way' between death and whipping.

d) **Australia was unknown and terrifying** – it had only been discovered in 1770! This would act as a deterrent to stop people from breaking the law.

e) **Transportation would help Britain to claim Australia** as part of its empire and stop countries like France from getting any of the land.

Activities

1 Why did transportation begin? Try to organise the reasons a) to e) visually: draw round your hand and write each reason on a finger. Put them in order of importance with the most important reason on the thumb.

2 Explain why you have put the reasons in that order. First practise your answer by explaining it to the person next to you. Start your explanations with connectives like 'This is the most important because …'; 'This was also important because …'

3 Look at the diagram at the top of this page. What sort of person was transported to Australia?

4 Why did the authorities choose not to punish other types of criminal this way?

4.5 Why did transportation end in the 1860s?

Transportation to Australia was clearly a punishment well used by the authorities. However, the last convict ship arrived in 1868, less than 100 years after the punishment began. So why did it end? The same factors you have seen earlier in this book will help you make sense of this sudden change.

Attitudes and beliefs

Roles of government

Poverty and wealth

Activities

1   Work in groups of three. Look at the sources and information on page 59 and organise them into the three categories below. Some of these may need their own category. Remember not all information is useful for every question.

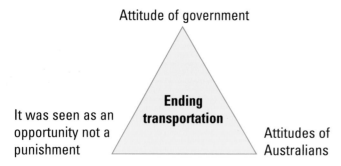

Attitude of government

Ending transportation

It was seen as an opportunity not a punishment

Attitudes of Australians

2   Each member of the group should choose one category and try to argue that theirs was the most important reason.

3   Decide which was the most important reason for ending transportation. Give reasons for your decision.

4   Which other factors are linked to the ending of this punishment? Explain your thinking.

Sources and information

The honest settlers in Australia set up groups to protest against transportation. They called it the 'stain' and demanded it be ended.

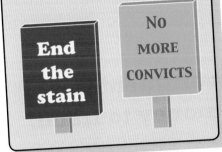

Source 1

In 1810, Lord Ellenborough said transportation was 'no more than a summer's excursion to a happier climate'.

Prisons were now cheaper and more widely used as a punishment. Transportation cost half a million pounds each year.

Source 2

Edward Carr, 1831, an official in Australia.

It is true that the convicts are sent out here as punishment. But it is equally true that it is not in the interests of the master to make his service a punishment but rather to make the condition of the convict as comfortable as he can afford. The interests of the master contradict the object of transportation.

By the 1850s Australia was established as British and no other country would claim it.

It is hard to find evidence of the impact of the anti-transportation campaign on the British government.

In 1851 gold was discovered in Australia. Many people tried to get tickets to travel to Australia during this 'gold rush'.

Transportation was a popular punishment with judges who often used it.

Source 3

Richard Dillingham dictated this letter to his parents, after being transported for taking part in protests in 1830.

As to my living I find it better than I ever expected thank God ... I want for nothing but my liberty but it is not the same with all that come as prisoners.

Many thought it unfair that prisoners who had won their ticket of leave could earn higher wages in Australia than in Britain.

Transportation was successful in reforming convicts. Many took the opportunity to stay out there and work peacefully. Only a minority ever came back to England. Crime had not fallen at all since this punishment began. In fact it had risen (as had the population).

By the 1850s, gaol for minor crimes was generally for less than a year. One year of gaol cost the government just £15 per prisoner. Seven to fourteen years of transportation cost on average £100 per prisoner.

4.6 How might changes to Britain have affected punishments?

After 1750 Britain changed almost beyond recognition. You can see some of the changes on these pages. The politicians brought in many new laws to try to respond to their rapidly changing society, hoping to maintain law and order in Britain. These two pages help you to understand the social changes that were taking place and how they affected crime and punishment.

Crimes

Huge increase in theft!

The government is losing money to fraud!

The 1860s saw the garrotting panic!

There are lots of protests and riots by the working class!

Range of punishments

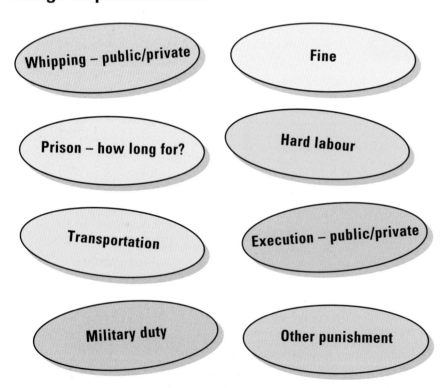

Whipping – public/private

Fine

Prison – how long for?

Hard labour

Transportation

Execution – public/private

Military duty

Other punishment

Activities

Work in groups. You are politicians in the 1800s and have to answer these questions:

1 Which crimes are increasing or causing concern?

2 Why is this happening? Look at the changes to society on page 61.

3 What are you going to do about it? What would be the right punishments for these crimes?

Give a presentation on your ideas.

The threat of revolution!

In 1789 there was a revolution in France. Many men and women died as ordinary people fought to gain the right to vote. MPs were worried that revolution might spread across the Channel, and were suspicious of any protest or demonstration – especially if it was about the right to vote.

Voting

In 1750 only a very small number of very rich men could vote. The only way people could make their voice heard was to hold a protest of some kind. In the 1800s 'suffrage' (the right to vote) was extended to include middle-class men. By 1885 nearly all men were able to vote.

Population growth

The population of England and Wales rose at an incredible rate. This caused huge worries – would the country be able to feed itself?
1750 – 9.5 million people
1900 – 41.5 million people

The British Empire

During the 1800s Britain took over many parts of the world.

The growth of towns

Towns grew across the country, where many people lived in awful conditions in large, anonymous slums. These slums, or 'rookeries', were a real worry for law makers in the 1800s. In 1851, for the first time, more people lived in towns than in villages.

Food prices

There had also been big changes to agriculture in Britain which meant more food was available, so bad harvests were not such a problem. By the 1800s food could also be imported from abroad if food was scarce. However the Corn Law was passed in 1815 to keep imported food prices high (and therefore keep profits high for landowners). This caused distress when British harvests were poor, especially for poorer people in towns. The Corn Law was abolished by Sir Robert Peel in 1846.

Changes to society

A revolution in industry

Developments in technology meant that there were huge changes in the workplace. Machines and factories meant that traditional skilled workers were often no longer needed because employers could hire cheaper, unskilled workers to run the machines, especially in the textile industry. Working conditions in factories could be incredibly dangerous, and children were expected to work in them as well as adults.

Taxation

The wars with France in the early 1800s meant that people were used to paying taxes. When the wars ended in 1815 the taxes remained, which meant the government could afford to spend more money on dealing with the problems of society.

Ideas and attitudes

In the 1700s there was a wave of thinking called the Enlightenment. This argued that the whole human race could improve itself through better living and working conditions, education and logical thought.

Later, after Charles Darwin developed his idea of evolution in the mid-1800s, some people thought that there was a criminal class that was less evolved than the rest of the population.

Young people

In 1750 only a minority of children went to school – the rest worked or had no job. Poor children often ended up in the workhouse, separated from their parents. Novels like Charles Dickens' *Oliver Twist* shows how some people worried that poor children might turn to crime. By 1880 the law said that all children up to the age of thirteen has to attend school.

4.7 How did punishment change in the 19th century?

You have seen the changes to British society – and these had a significant effect on the way people were punished. The government took a more active role in running punishments, most notably prisons. How did this affect the way people were punished?

Roles of government

The 1815 Gaol Act could be seen as a turning point – the government now took responsibility for the wages of those working in prisons. Many new ideas came in the decades that followed. However, changes were slow to take root and old punishments like the pillory were still occasionally used.

Fear of crime was still an important factor – scares like the garrotting crisis of the 1860s could lead the authorities to make prison terms longer and conditions harsher.

Key dates	Development
1777	John Howard's book, *The State of Prisons in England and Wales*, published
1815	Gaolers paid by taxes
1820	Whipping ended for women
1832	Executed prisoners could no longer be given up for dissection
1835	First prison inspectors appointed
1837	Pillory no longer used
1839	Rules the same across all prisons
1842	New model prison built at Pentonville, London
1857	Hulks (prison ships) no longer used
1862	Public whipping ended
1863	Men in prison could receive up to 50 strokes of the whip. Electric shocks also introduced
1868	Public execution ended
1868	Transportation ended
1872	Stocks no longer used
1878	Government took control of all prisons

Source 1

▲ Engraving by William Hogarth from 1751 showing an executed prisoner being dissected. In 1832 this was no longer allowed.

Case study: the Chartists

A look at the punishments handed out to the Chartists in the 1830s and 40s allows us to see if there had mainly been continuity in punishments, or if a great deal had changed. The Chartists were an organisation trying to win the right to vote, and were regularly suppressed by the government. The evidence on this page should give you a good idea of the punishments they received.

Activities

1 Draw up a table to gather information about change and continuity. Look at the information about the Chartists and see if it shows change or continuity. You may wish to look at pages 50–51 again to refresh your knowledge about punishments in the 18th century.

Evidence	Change – new punishments used	Continuity – old-fashioned punishments used

2 Decide if you agree with the following statements – give reasons for your answers.
   a) Punishments changed more than they stayed the same.
   b) Punishments were less harsh than they used to be.
   c) Punishments became less public in the 1800s.
   d) Punishments became fairer in the 1800s.
   e) Prisons were used more than they had been before.

3 The Chartists were punished for their protests. Does this mean you can generalise about **all** punishments from their example? Look at the key dates and find out when the following punishments ended: whipping, pillory, public execution, transportation.

4 Some historians describe the changes in punishment as being 'from public to private'. Do you agree?

Phineas Smithers received 18 months' hard labour for rioting in Bradford.

William Lovett received 12 months in prison for 'seditious libel'.

Feargus O'Connor received 18 months in gaol for writing provocative articles.

Ernest Jones was put in solitary confinement when in gaol, for refusing to work.

Ishmael Evans received three years in prison for 'administering illegal oaths'.

John Marshall, a knife maker from Sheffield, was sentenced to two years' hard labour for rioting.

Charles Davis, 26, was sentenced to 18 months in Chester gaol for 'conspiracy'.

How were the Chartists punished?

The son of a slave, **William Cuffay** was a London tailor and organiser of a huge meeting in London in 1848. He also sometimes spoke in favour of using force to achieve the vote. He was charged with treason and transported to Australia for life.

Almost 1,500 Chartists were arrested following riots in 1842, known as the **Plug Plots**. Two people and one soldier died at Salterhebble in Halifax as a result, and 79 Chartists were found guilty and faced sentences including:

- execution
- 7–21 years in prison
- transportation to Australia.

John Frost was leader of the **Newport Rising** in 1839 – a Chartist protest that led to 22 deaths. He and the two other leaders were the last people to be sentenced to be hanged, drawn and quartered. Following a public outcry, this was reduced to transportation for life. He was given a full pardon in 1854 and returned home.

Thirty Chartists, including three women, were arrested after the **Llanidloes rising** of 1839–40. Three men were transported – the rest mainly received short gaol terms.

4.8 Why was there a revolution in prisons during the Industrial Revolution?

As you have seen, prisons were increasingly used in the 1800s. But why did the government need to take over running them? What were the problems with prisons at the time? One man, John Howard, published an influential book in 1777 demonstrating just how terrible conditions were. John Howard and Elizabeth Fry both dedicated themselves to visiting prisons across the country, and both believed that prisons should reform criminals. How did this lead to a revolution in prisons?

Key individuals

Activity

It is 1783. Sir George Paul wants to build a new prison in Gloucester and has asked you, John Howard, to prepare a report on the state of prisons. He wants to know what the main problems are – and how you would solve them.

Investigate the evidence on pages 64–67 and copy and complete the following table:

Problem	Evidence	Explanation: why was this a problem?	Solution
Poverty and wealth			
Hygiene and health			
Mixed prisoners			

Source 1

Criminals convicted of minor offences	16%
Serious offenders awaiting trial, transportation or execution	24.3%
Debtors	59.7%

▲ John Howard found out the reasons why people were held in prisons.

Source 2

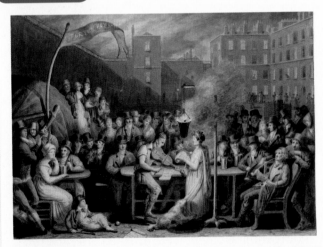

◀ Wealthy inmates enjoying a luxurious lifestyle in King's Bench Prison, London, 1805. There was little that could not be obtained by the rich – pigs were only banned from being kept in Newgate Gaol in 1714!

Source 3

This prisoner gave evidence to Parliament about conditions in York Gaol.

All sorts of characters were together. There was much talk about crime and instructing one another in all manner of wickedness. The effect of all this was to make a man ten times worse than before and he would be sure to return to a life of crime.

Source 5

William Smith visited Middlesex prisons in 1776 and said he saw 'vagrants and disorderly women of the very lowest and most wretched class of human beings, almost naked and with only a few filthy rags, almost alive with vermin'.

Source 4

Fees charged at Nottingham prison in 1760:

Paid to the warder on release – 13s 4d
Paid to the turnkey on release – 1s 4d

Prison warders were not paid by the government. They earned their money by charging prisoners fees for rooms, food and anything else that was needed. Fees were also charged for seeing doctors.

Source 6

a) Salaries:
Gaoler £0
Surgeon £0
Chaplain £40

b) Prisoners:
Debtors 16
Criminals 24

c) Accommodation
Day room for men and women criminals:
3.5 x 2 metres
Day room for debtors: 6 x 2 metres
No window
Part of the wall broken to allow
ventilation and light

d) Deaths:
Many died in 1773.
Eight died at Christmas
of smallpox.

THE RULES OF THE ROOM
EVERY MAN THAT COME IN TO
PAY 3d FOR COLS STICKS
AND CANDLES

k) In prisons
where debtors
mixed with
serious criminals,
the warders let
the criminals
have the same
privileges as the
debtors. There
were not enough
warders to keep
them separate.

e) Many prisoners who had been
found not guilty could not get out
of prison because they could not
afford the discharge [release] fee.

f) Five or six children
have lately been
born in the gaol.

j) Prisoners
already in a
cell forced new
prisoners to
pay a fee to
them known
as a garnish.
Warders did
little to stop
this.

i) At Abingdon the floor
swarmed with vermin and
eight women were in irons.

CHANDLER

SOAP

h) The prisoners could
not be chained or forced
to work. In Marshalsea
prison in London,
butchers and other
tradesmen came into
the prison to sell food
or play skittles with the
prisoners in the prison
drinking room.

g) A chandler had four rooms in the
[Marshalsea] prison. He used one as his
workroom and shop, two for his family and
sub-let the last room to other prisoners.

▲ Text from John Howard's book, *The State of Prisons in England and Wales*, published in 1777. All boxes
except h), i) and j) describe conditions in Gloucester Gaol.

What impact could one woman have?

Look at a five pound note. On the back of it you will see a picture of a woman. That woman is Elizabeth Fry, a young lady who lived in the 1800s and changed women's prisons greatly. On these pages you will find details about her life. Your task is to decide just how **significant** she was.

What Elizabeth found on visiting Newgate Gaol, London in 1813:

- Men and women were mixed together sometimes
- Conditions were overcrowded – 300 in one room
- Some women worked as prostitutes in jail to afford food
- Many babies were born inside prison
- Women prisoners were sometimes whipped.

Activity

Write a biography of Elizabeth Fry. You should include sections on key features from her life:
- Her early life
- What beliefs influenced her actions
- What she did in Newgate
- Her long-term impact – how significant was she?

Source 1

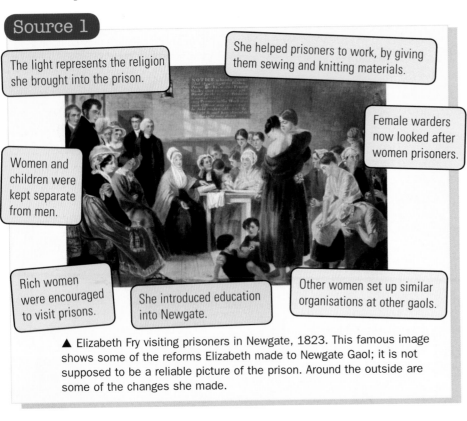

The light represents the religion she brought into the prison.

She helped prisoners to work, by giving them sewing and knitting materials.

Female warders now looked after women prisoners.

Women and children were kept separate from men.

Rich women were encouraged to visit prisons.

She introduced education into Newgate.

Other women set up similar organisations at other gaols.

▲ Elizabeth Fry visiting prisoners in Newgate, 1823. This famous image shows some of the reforms Elizabeth made to Newgate Gaol; it is not supposed to be a reliable picture of the prison. Around the outside are some of the changes she made.

Source 3

The aims of the Association for the Reformation of Female Prisoners in Newgate

… to provide for the clothing, the instruction, and the employment of these females, to introduce them to knowledge of the holy scriptures, and to form in them as much as lies in our power, those habits of order, sobriety, and industry which may render them docile and perceptible whilst in prison, and respectable when they leave it.

Source 4

Elizabeth Fry's attitude to punishment

Punishment is not for revenge, but to lessen crime and reform the criminal.

Source 2

Elizabeth Fry, writing a letter to her young children, 1813

I have lately been twice to Newgate to see after the poor prisoners who had poor little infants without clothing, or with very little and I think if you saw how small a piece of bread they are each allowed a day you would be very sorry.

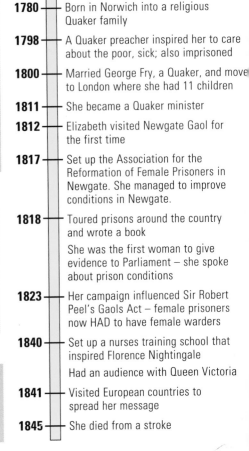

1780	Born in Norwich into a religious Quaker family
1798	A Quaker preacher inspired her to care about the poor, sick; also imprisoned
1800	Married George Fry, a Quaker, and moved to London where she had 11 children
1811	She became a Quaker minister
1812	Elizabeth visited Newgate Gaol for the first time
1817	Set up the Association for the Reformation of Female Prisoners in Newgate. She managed to improve conditions in Newgate.
1818	Toured prisons around the country and wrote a book. She was the first woman to give evidence to Parliament – she spoke about prison conditions
1823	Her campaign influenced Sir Robert Peel's Gaols Act – female prisoners now HAD to have female warders
1840	Set up a nurses training school that inspired Florence Nightingale. Had an audience with Queen Victoria
1841	Visited European countries to spread her message
1845	She died from a stroke

Changes to prisons in the 1800s

John Howard's book influenced a reform movement and many changes to prisons were made in the 1800s. In 1896 the aim of prisons was summed up as 'the humanisation of the individual and training for freedom' – a huge change from the prisons John Howard visited a century earlier. You can see pictures of the new prisons here; they show the effects of reforms. But exactly what reforms had been made?

Activities

1 Look carefully at the sources. Make some key notes on:

a) what prison life was like in the 1800s

b) what reforms had been made

PRISONS

c) why the changes had been made

d) what hadn't been reformed

2 There were arguments about whether to keep prisoners totally separate, or just silent. Which sources do you think reflect the **separate** system and which reflect the **silent** system?

3 There were also debates about whether prisoners should do useful or pointless work. Which sources reflect **pointless** work?

Source 1

▲ Prisoners at exercise. Each is wearing a face mask with a long, low peak, and holds a rope with knots at 4.5m intervals.

Source 2

▲ This prison chapel has been specially constructed so that each prisoner is boxed in, only able to see the preacher and the guards.

Source 3

▲ The crank. Prisoners had to turn this wheel a certain number of times to earn their next meal.

Source 4

▲ The treadmill was seen by some as hard labour – one magistrate called it 'an engine of terrible oppression'.

Source 5

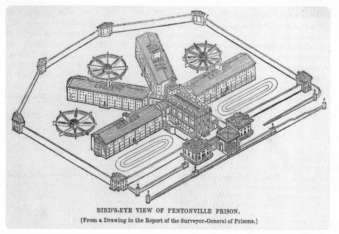

BIRD'S-EYE VIEW OF PENTONVILLE PRISON.
(From a Drawing in the Report of the Surveyor-General of Prisons.)

▲ This purpose-built prison is solid and secure, with quite large cells – 4.5m x 3.5m, each with a washbasin and barred window. The design, like spokes around a wheel hub, gave warders a clear view of a whole wing of the prison from the central area.

These prisons are still the basis of Britain's prison system today, although often now with two prisoners in cells designed for one.

4.9 How did the punishment of women change?

How does a historian find out about punishments? Even just ten years ago this would have involved months of research in a dusty archive, painstakingly making notes and reading hundreds of sources. Advances in technology mean that many archives are now available online and searches that would have taken many weeks can be done in seconds! You too can carry out this work, and perhaps make important discoveries.

A good example is the Old Bailey archive at www.oldbaileyonline.org where the evidence on this page was uncovered. This online archive contains the records of all the trials at the Old Bailey courthouse in London between 1674 and 1913. By searching the archive we can discover the interesting statistic that only 14 per cent of all the people found guilty were woman. What more can we find out if we investigate further?

Activities

1 Match the possible punishments to the crimes on page 69. NB Some punishments apply to more than one crime.

2 What does each punishment tell us about the way women were treated?

3 How did the punishment of minor property crimes such as theft change in the 1800s?

4 Look at Source 1. What changing patterns can you see in the punishments given to women? What new questions do you need answered to help you understand these patterns better?

5 Go to the Old Bailey online website. Use the search facility to find out more about women and crime.

The key questions you will be trying to answer are:

a) What sort of crimes did women carry out?

b) What sort of punishments did women receive?

c) Did the punishments change in the 1800s?

Women and the law

- Women could not be lawyers, magistrates or even part of normal juries. Special women-only juries were put together if a woman was sentenced to death but claimed she was pregnant.

- The law of Feme Covert meant that a woman could not be convicted if her husband was present at the crime – it was presumed he was giving her the orders!

Source 1

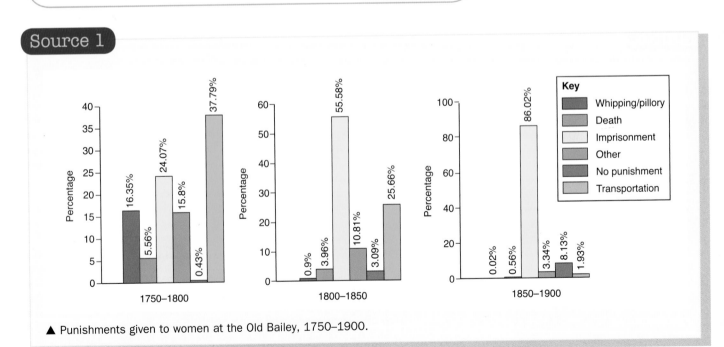

▲ Punishments given to women at the Old Bailey, 1750–1900.

Crimes

1727

Mary Mukes and Jane Dennis

Highway robbery: They got a man drunk on gin, then robbed him on the highway

1789

Sarah Acton

Theft: stole some young pigs

1815

Mary Blake, Elizabeth Smith, Elizabeth Lambert

Theft: shoplifting, 63 yards of cotton

1837

Mary Dobson

Theft: a pair of boots

1865

Mary Ann West

Theft: pickpocketing one wallet

1891

Annie Cook

Concealing the birth of her child

1891

Mary Pulbrook

Theft: a watch and chain

1700

Rebecca Maud

Theft: burglary (repeat offender)

1827

Rosina Smith

Theft: watch and gold chain

1674

Mall Floyd

Theft and kidnap of children

1674

Elizabeth Flower

Petty treason: murdering her husband with a poker (he had attacked her with the poker)

Possible punishments

A Branding

B Transportation (7 years)

C Death

D Prison (3 days)

E Transportation

F Prison (9 months)

G Prison + 9 months' hard labour

H Prison (2 days)

4.10 Did prisons change more in the 19th or 20th century?

There was a huge amount of change to prisons in the 20th century. For example the prison population halved in the 1910s–30s as more people were put on probation – but did this trend continue? Just as you have done for young offenders on pages 2–5, you need to look at the evidence about adult punishments in the 20th century, and be able to compare them to changes in previous centuries.

Activities

1 Work in small groups. Look at the sources and information on pages 70–73 and create a memory map on prison life. Organise your information into these branches:
   - work and education
   - living conditions
   - staff
   - safety.

2 Read the information then prepare a short presentation answering the question:

   'Did prisons change more in the 20th century than in the 19th century?'

   One half of your group will argue that the 20th century saw the more significant change; the other half will argue for the 19th century.

Look back at pages 64–67 for changes to prisons made in the 19th century, and look at pages 70–71 for changes made in the 20th century.

Source 1

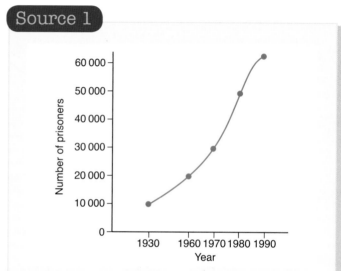

▲ The rising prison population in the 20th century. By January 2010 the prison population had climbed to just over 83,300. In November 2010, 5% of the prison population was female.

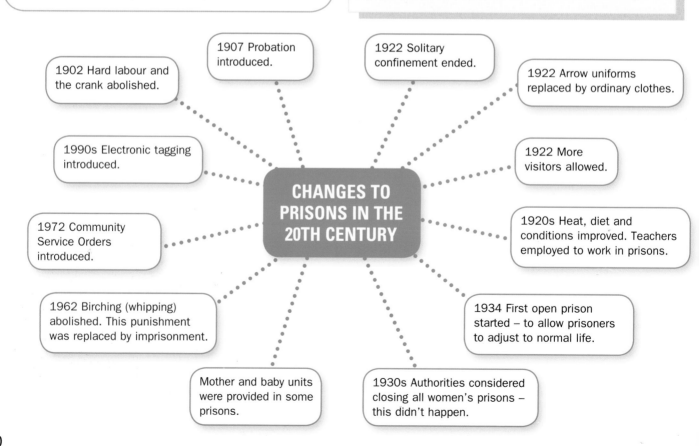

1902 Hard labour and the crank abolished.

1907 Probation introduced.

1922 Solitary confinement ended.

1922 Arrow uniforms replaced by ordinary clothes.

1990s Electronic tagging introduced.

1922 More visitors allowed.

1972 Community Service Orders introduced.

1920s Heat, diet and conditions improved. Teachers employed to work in prisons.

1962 Birching (whipping) abolished. This punishment was replaced by imprisonment.

1934 First open prison started – to allow prisoners to adjust to normal life.

Mother and baby units were provided in some prisons.

1930s Authorities considered closing all women's prisons – this didn't happen.

CHANGES TO PRISONS IN THE 20TH CENTURY

Increasing prison population

Sentences have become longer – ten years is now a common sentence; in the past it was unusual.

Prisoners on remand have increased – these are prisoners waiting for their trial. Some wait up to a year, even though they haven't been found guilty yet.

Attitudes have changed – some crimes are punished more severely. Three times more drunk drivers were sent to prison in 1990 than 1980. The proportion of thieves sent to prison (rather than having other sentences) went up by 25 per cent in just seven years after 1977.

1

Overcrowding

Overcrowding in prisons has became a serious problem. Leeds Prison was designed to hold 624 people – but in 1981 it housed 1,200, with many sharing cells designed for one! It had sixteen baths and three showers – but water could only be used for four baths at once.

2

Source 2

▲ A prison ship used in the 1990s to hold 500 prisoners. It was moored off the Dorset coast, not far from where hulks would have been used 200 years earlier.

Riots

In some prisons overcrowding and staff shortages meant prisoners could be in their cells for as much as 23 hours a day. Education programmes to reform prisoners were also cut. This meant that tensions mounted and serious prison riots occurred, for example at Strangeways in Manchester in 1990 – riots which caused millions of pounds worth of damages.

3

Private prisons

One solution was to build more prisons, and in the 1990s private companies were allowed to build and run prisons for the first time since the 1800s. They operate under strict rules from the government and each has a controller linked directly to the Ministry of Justice. There are currently 11 privately run prisons in the UK.

4

Substance abuse

One-third of prisoners have severe alcohol problems, but in 2004 only one prison had an alcohol abuse programme to help. Drugs are also a serious problem inside prisons, with few drug rehabilitation programmes available. In a crackdown in 2005, £140,000 worth of drugs were confiscated in Norwich Prison alone! A 2004 study found that over 12 per cent of prisoners tested had drugs in their system.

5

Source 3

▲ Rioters at Strangeways, 1990.

Did prisons change more in the 20th century than in the 19th century?

Life in modern prisons

Remember you are still gathering evidence about changes to prisons. Evidence from prisoners is certainly going to be very useful for historians investigating this topic. On these pages you can find evidence from two very different ex-convicts.

Erwin James' first brush with the law came at the age of 11, when he was in a care home. He served 20 years of a life sentence for the robbery and murder of two men. While in jail he studied for and obtained a History degree and is now an author and advisor to the Prison Reform Trust.

John Hoskisson was a professional golfer who was convicted of manslaughter for killing a cyclist by drink-driving. He was sent to prison for three years.

Source 1

It made me think about some of the people I had met inside. There was Dave, who on the outside had been a postman; Howard, who had been a student; and Tam who had been a council worker. The four of us played pool at the weekend. Tam was the captain of the wing football team, nicknamed 'the Commander' for his prowess in midfield. Dave had asthma so he'd taken up jogging. He'd lost two stone, bolstered his health and begun doing sponsored runs around the football pitch for charity. Howard spent his days in the education department studying and dreaming of becoming a teacher.

A stream of denim-clad men in identical blue-and-white-striped shirts are shuffling past my door. I step out and join the flux. Down two flights of metal stairs to the ground floor; we're headed towards a set of trestle tables. A row of prisoners in white are serving food. Before I get there I am stopped in my tracks by a scream: 'He's f– dead meat!' 'Nonce! He's f– dead meat!' I turn and see two men: one wields a mop handle, the other a metal bucket. They are using the domestic implements to beat a third prisoner who cowers in a cell doorway. 'He's f– dead meat!'

Suddenly I'm aware that no one else is stopping. Nobody is intervening. Few even look in the direction of the violence. I fall back in line, pick up a tray, collect my meal and return to my cell. As I sit on the chair and spoon down the food, all thoughts and feelings about why I am in prison are relegated. My first priority, I now understand, is to learn to survive.

Back in the chapel, a prisoner was telling the [visiting] judge that life inside was 'a war of survival'. I recognised the angry voice instantly: it was John, who lives on my spur. The same John who a few months earlier had led an attempt to burn a number of sex offenders. John's accomplice had been transferred out of the prison following the riot but he had remained, his status with other prisoners enhanced.

Prison can work, but not if the system is overloaded and under-resourced. And if it is to work in society's best interest, it is imperative that only those that really need to be locked up, are, and that all prisons work towards a positive regime where respect and dignity for inmates is not compromised for misguided reasons.

▲ Extracts from James' column for the *Guardian* newspaper in 2003.

Source 2

Wandsworth

'The cell door flew open and three of Wandsworth's most feared warders charged in.

'Against the wall,' they screamed, truncheons drawn. For a split second there was pandemonium but in that time I saw Jimmy Baker, one of my cellmates, whip a small parcel of heroin out of his pocket and swallow it.

Minutes later we were all back in the cell – the beds had been overturned, mattresses split open, pictures ripped off the wall and the sheets left in a pile on the dirty stone floor.

Later Jimmy picked up his slop bucket and with practised ease retched up the contents of his stomach including the parcel of heroin he had swallowed. I told him I'd have to ask to have him moved out if he smoked heroin. 'Do that and I'll knife you,' he said.

I've never been so fearful of my own safety. As the night progressed he became more volatile, screaming obscenities. Sleep was impossible and I could not disengage my mind from the terror of my incarceration with this loathsome, drug-crazed creature.

Coldingley

The bonus of a C-category prison is being allowed to wear one's own clothes; the downside, was that because inmates were supposedly more trustworthy, officers left each prison landing unsupervised. Consequently the place was filthy. Stale mouldy food littered the floor, dustbins overflowed, and the windows were so dirty hardly any light filtered through.

In Wandsworth only small radios had been allowed, but here everyone seemed to have huge ghetto blasters. The noise was excruciating. The thin walls of my cell shut out none of the noise and it drowned my radio set at full volume. That first night I managed to sleep only after the walls stopped shaking at 2a.m. One night at two o'clock I lost my rag. 'Turn down that racket,' I screamed. The reply was immediate and ominous: 'You're going to get it whitey.' For the next few days I lived in fear and spent my free time holed up in my cell. Complaining wasn't an option. Over the next year I saw many horrific incidents that arose solely because of the intolerable noise level and the unwillingness of those who ran the prison to do anything about it.

The next day at last was my first induction – setting objectives for each prisoner. I'd been in Wandsworth for weeks but had never been introduced to this process every prisoner is supposed to undergo. I asked for education opportunities and to keep fit in the gym. I was to be disappointed. The gym was minute and decrepit with gaping holes in the floorboards. As for education, because of savage budget cuts, only 20 out of 280 inmates were on courses. No trades were taught. GCSE English was the most advanced course you could take.

Everyone at Coldingley was expected to work. I was assigned to the metal shop. The whole thing was farcical. After a cursory explanation, the supervisor left me at my huge pressing machine with just the comment: 'Do the best you can.' It took me five minutes to learn the job. Ten minutes to invent a quicker way of doing it. Fifteen before I received a warning: 'Hey you – you're working too hard.' At the end of the first week we had produced 2000 pieces; 1800 had to be scrapped because they'd been badly made.

Every week I saw prisoners released back into the outside world with nothing to show for their time inside except a £46 discharge grant. Regularly they were rearrested within days.

Conclusions

It's been a real eye-opener, prison. Perhaps it's now time I made some sort of comment. One thing's for certain – prison is essential. There are some dangerous people in here; the public has a right to be protected. But it's no good putting everyone in the same boat. There are good prisoners ... and someone has got to do something about the problem of drugs. An ever-increasing proportion of the 60,000 angry men in prison will be getting out hooked on heroin and looking for revenge.

▲ Extracts from Hoskisson's book *Inside.*

Activity

Make two lists from James' and Hoskisson's extracts: **a)** problems with prisons and **b)** good things about prisons. This will help you build your evidence base for your main question: Did prisons change more in the 20th century than in the 19th century? Go back to page 70 if you need to check what this enquiry is about.

4.11 Why did the death penalty end in 1965?

The death penalty had been used as a punishment less and less since the end of the Bloody Code. In this section you will be investigating the end of the death penalty, and the attitudes that lay behind this great change.

On 13 August 1964, at precisely 8a.m., two men, in two different prisons, had white hoods placed over their heads, their ankles strapped and their feet placed onto a chalk mark on a wooden trapdoor. Seconds later they were dead. The time from trapdoor opening to death was momentary – the length of the rope was calculated carefully and the knot was placed precisely on their neck to ensure the spine snapped instantly. The clock was still chiming eight.

These two men, Peter Allen and Gwynne Evans, both convicted of murder, were the last two people to be executed in the United Kingdom. In 1965 a law was passed abolishing capital punishment for five years. It has remained abolished ever since.

But why 1965 and not at any other time? This is what you will be investigating. Putting it very simply, the pendulum of opinion had swung away from the death penalty. But as you can see below two main factors need to be considered:

Factors

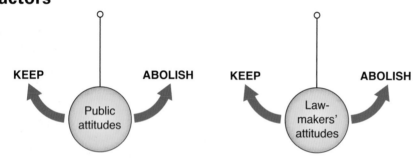

FACT: Capital punishment had police support.

Source 1

Lord Templewood was in favour of capital punishment when he was Home Secretary. However, by the 1960s he had changed his mind – visiting countries like Switzerland convinced him that murderers could be reformed.

FACT: From 1900 to 1924 an average of 14 people were executed each year. By the 1960s this was 1–2 per year.

FACT: Some juries were reluctant to convict people if they felt the punishment was too harsh.

FACT: Many people still wanted the 'ultimate' deterrent.

Source 2

Reginald Paget MP speaking in Parliament in 1947.

Let the dictators have their gallows and their axes, their firing squads and their lethal chambers. We, the citizens of a free democracy, do not have to shelter under the shadow of the gallows tree.

Activities

1 Look at the sources and information on these pages. Decide which factor it fits into. For example, Source 1 matches law makers' attitudes.

2 Decide if it suggests the pendulum was swinging towards keeping or abolishing capital punishment. For example, would you put Source 1 on the 'Keep capital punishment' side or on the 'Abolish' side?

3 Overall, which factor was the most important in swinging the pendulum of opinion and ending capital punishment?

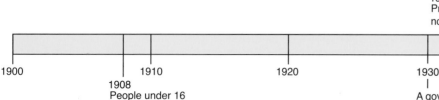

74

Source 3

The Times newspaper.

1922 In favour of capital punishment
1947 Against capital punishment

Source 4

The Judge Gerald Gardiner, who later became Lord Chancellor, wrote a letter showing that 21 countries had abolished the death penalty and murder rates had not gone up. He also asked if there was 'something so particularly brutal about Englishmen that they need a special form of deterrent that nearly every civilised country has found ... to be ... unnecessary'.

Source 5

Albert Pierrepoint was one of Britain's last official executioners. He hanged over 430 criminals, including Nazis after World War II and Ruth Ellis, the last woman to be hanged.

I have come to the conclusion that executions solve nothing ... it did not deter them then and it had not deterred them when they committed what they were convicted for. All the men and women I have faced at that final moment convince me that in what I have done I have not prevented a single murder.

Source 6

In 1953, 50 MPs signed a motion asking the Home Secretary to show clemency to Derek Bentley and cancel his execution. One MP was so angry he said 'Is the House [of Parliament] to wait until Bentley is dead before it is entitled to say that he should not die?'

FACT: Some people thought it was an un-Christian punishment.

FACT: In Holland, the murder rate fell after they abolished the death penalty.

Key individual: Derek Bentley

The tragic case of Derek Bentley in 1953 made people think very carefully about the death penalty. His execution did not mean capital punishment ended overnight, but the case received a huge level of publicity with many newspapers suggesting the current system was outdated and inconsistent. But was there anything special about his case?

- He was found guilty of murder, after a policeman was shot in Croydon.
- The shot was fired by Derek's friend Chris Craig – but he was only 16 and too young to be hanged.
- Derek was already being restrained by a policeman when the shot was fired.
- He was found guilty of murder because he shouted 'let him have it'.
- Derek Bentley had a mental age of 11.
- The jury had recommended mercy but the judge did not change the sentence.
- Thousands of people signed a petition demanding mercy, but the Home Secretary refused to change the sentence.
- Derek Bentley was hanged on 28 January 1953, aged 19.
- The campaign did not end in 1953, and in 1998 the Court of Appeal agreed the verdict was wrong and Derek's name was finally cleared.

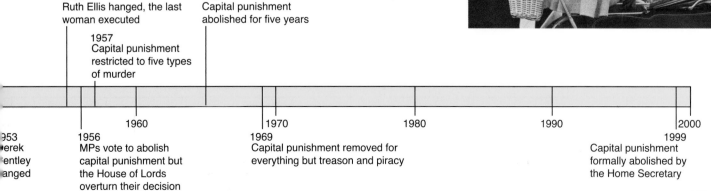

1953
Derek Bentley hanged

1955
Ruth Ellis hanged, the last woman executed

1956
MPs vote to abolish capital punishment but the House of Lords overturn their decision

1957
Capital punishment restricted to five types of murder

1960

1965
Capital punishment abolished for five years

1969
Capital punishment removed for everything but treason and piracy

1970

1980

1990

1999
Capital punishment formally abolished by the Home Secretary

2000

4.12 **Could one event change punishments completely?**

In July 2005 four young men travelled to London and detonated bombs in a co-ordinated terror attack that killed 52 innocent people. They set off their bombs on three Tube trains and a bus as people made their way to work. The four young men were all British, and inspired by the terrorist group Al Qaeda. This enquiry does not investigate why they carried out their attack, but you will be expected to look at how their actions affected laws and attitudes after the attacks happened.

Some of the events you have studied are in the distant past. The 2005 bombings are very recent. Some of you may have friends or family who were caught up in the bombs. The fear it created is still present in many people's minds. However, remember you are a historian and must look at the evidence with a historian's mind. The activities on these pages will lead you to answer one **big** question:

What changed after the July bombings?

Source 2

▲ The remains of the bus at Tavistock Square, London. Thirteen innocent people died on this bus.

Source 1

▲ Map showing the location of the London bombings.

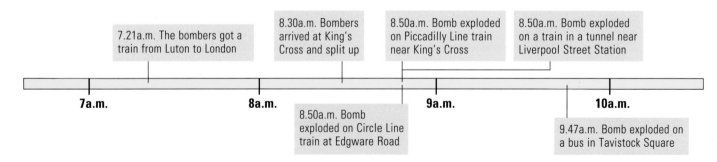

7.21a.m. The bombers got a train from Luton to London

8.30a.m. Bombers arrived at King's Cross and split up

8.50a.m. Bomb exploded on Piccadilly Line train near King's Cross

8.50a.m. Bomb exploded on a train in a tunnel near Liverpool Street Station

7a.m. 8a.m. 9a.m. 10a.m.

8.50a.m. Bomb exploded on Circle Line train at Edgware Road

9.47a.m. Bomb exploded on a bus in Tavistock Square

Context: other terrorist bombings by Al Qaeda-inspired groups

- 11 September 2001 – 2,973 people were killed in co-ordinated attacks in America, including hijacking planes and flying into the Twin Towers in New York.
- 12 October 2002 – 202 people were killed following an attack on the holiday island of Bali, Indonesia.
- 11 March 2004 – 191 people were killed in the Madrid train bombings.
- 21 July 2005 – Terrorists failed to set off four bombs in London. No link has ever been proven to the 7 July terrorists.

The 4 Ps – how the security services deal with terrorist threats

PREVENT – strategies to stop people joining radical extremists and terrorists

PURSUE – finding ways to disrupt and bring to justice terrorist networks

PROTECT – providing security advice and protection from physical and electronic attack

PREPARE – risk assessments that work out potential responses to a threat.

Control orders

Control orders are special powers that the Home Secretary gained in March 2005, several months before the bombs. This means that, where there is only secret evidence, terror suspects can have their liberty restricted and never see the evidence for this. Some people think this law contradicts Human Rights Laws. In December 2006 there were 16 people affected by control orders. Possible restrictions include:

- house arrest
- electronic tagging
- handing over passport
- limits on who they can see.

Protests

In April 2005 a law was passed banning protests outside the Houses of Parliament.

Source 3

From the official government 'Intelligence and Security Committee Report' into the bombings, 2006. The numbers are blacked out under the Official Secrets Act.

We record that *** terrorist plots in the UK have been thwarted by the intelligence and security agencies since 11 September 2001, three of them since July 2005. Despite their successes disrupting these other plots, they did not manage to prevent the attacks that took place in London on 7 July 2005 ...

... We have been struck by the sheer scale of the problem that our intelligence and security agencies face and their comparatively small capacity to cover it.

Activities

Read the case files on this page and answer the questions.

1 What happened on 7 July 2005?

2 Was the bombing a one-off event or does the evidence suggest that it was part of a wider situation? What information supports your point of view?

3 How had laws been changing **before** the bombings happened? What could explain this?

Could one event change punishments completely?

2006 Terrorism Act

In 2006 the government passed a new law on terrorism. It was drawn up as a response to the July bombings. Some of the key points were:

Crime	Punishment (maximum)
Encouraging terrorism	7 years
Training for terrorism	10 years
Preparing a terrorist act	Life
Using radioactive materials	Life

Activities

You have read what happened on 7 July 2005, and some of the context of the crime. But how did it affect punishments – and what do people's attitude to the crime tell us?

1 Organise the changes since the July bombings into these categories:
 a) changes that have increased freedom and safety
 b) changes that have limited freedom and safety.

2 Work in threes. One of you has to argue that the information and sources on these pages support 1a) more than it does 1b). Another person has to argue that the information and sources supports 1b) more than it does 1a). The third person has to decide who argues their point of view more persuasively. Swap roles until you have all tried each task.

3 Do you think the changes to punishments would have happened without the bombs on 7 July? Explain your answer.

Changes

Government initiatives and changes after the July bombings

- The police set up three new regional Counter-Terrorism Units in England, which work closely with MI5.
- Re-organisation of the security services' IT systems.
- Closer links between MI6 and the Pakistan security services.
- £85 million extra given to security services in December 2005.
- A careful change in the way police speak to people.
- Funding for 200 community projects aimed at preventing violent extremism; for example citizenship education programmes in mosque schools and funding youth offender panels.
- A new police PREVENT plan, with £11 million for 300 new PREVENT officers.
- A programme to tackle radicalisation in prisons.

Convictions

Convictions under anti-terror laws:
2007 – 36 people
2008 – 32 people

Detention

Since the 2006 Act, terror suspects can be held for up to 28 days without being charged. For normal crimes the time limit is usually only 24 hours. Originally the government wanted the period to be up to 90 days, but MPs reduced it to 28.

In October 2005 the police gave some reasons why they wanted to be able to detain terror suspects for longer:

Modern terrorists try to maximise casualties so must be stopped early – evidence will be harder to find.

CCTV footage and mobile phone data may take many weeks rather than days to search through.

Suspects use fake identities and these take time to be traced.

Computers and other modern technology make it easy to encrypt evidence, which takes a long time to find.

Terrorists act globally so evidence needs to be gathered from around the world.

Forensic scientists need time to analyse the evidence.

Activities

Finally you should look at the attitudes people held at the time.

4 How did people react to the changes after the bombings? Look at people's attitudes and see what they tell us about:
  a) attitudes of the government
  b) attitudes of ordinary people
  c) any attitudes that link to question 1 on page 78.

5 Do you think the changes to punishment and new laws were more about an increased threat from terrorism or about an increased fear of crime? Explain your answer.

Source 1

Prime Minister Tony Blair, 7 July 2005.

It's important, however, that those engaged in terrorism realise that our determination to defend our values and our way of life is greater than their determination to cause death and destruction to innocent people.

Source 2

A comment by the free speech organisation Liberty.

What more fertile recruitment ground for extremism could there be than innocent young men released without charge after 90 days' internment?

Source 3

The *Guardian* newspaper, 2005

It is a huge breach of the 300-year-old habeas corpus principle that every arrested citizen has a right to be either charged or freed. Democracies are not supposed to allow imprisonment without trial.

Source 4

The *Sun* newspaper, 2005

Attempts to strengthen the hand of our police against terrorists are under attack. 'Human rights' champions, woolly MPs and leftie judges want to scrap plans for holding terror suspects without charge for 90 days.

Source 5

The Director General of the security service, 2003.

The nature of counter-terrorism is to get ahead of the game to stop, frustrate or otherwise prevent terrorist activity. That is the primary goal but the reality is that we can never stop all such attacks and no security intelligence organisation in the world could do so. An attack may get through our defences.

Source 6

The reaction of London Mayor Ken Livingstone.

This was not a terrorist attack against the mighty and the powerful. It was not aimed at presidents or prime ministers. It was aimed at ordinary working-class Londoners, black and white, Muslim and Christian, Hindu and Jew, young and old. Indiscriminate slaughter irrespective of any consideration for age, class, religion, whatever.

Source 7

Sir Iqbal Sacranie, the Muslim Council of Great Britain.

What we need to be aware of is that the terrorists, these evil people who have carried out this series of explosions in London, want to demoralise us as a nation and divide us as a people. All of us must unite in helping the police to hunt these murderers down.

Source 8

The head of MI5, 2007.

We will do our utmost to hold back the physical threat of attacks but, alone, this is merely containment. Long-term resolution requires identifying and addressing the root causes of the problem.

The impression that John Howard gave of prisons (see page 65) was very accurate. The conditions he described in 1777 in the gaols of England and Wales were appalling. But does that mean that Howard deserves most of the credit for improving these conditions?

This Exam Buster contains important advice on questions that ask you to analyse and explain the importance of an individual. It models how to approach the question if a student chose to write about John Howard's impact on prison reform.

---

2 The boxes below show two important individuals.

Choose **one** individual and explain why that person was important in changing attitudes about punishment.

John Howard and his book 'The State of Prisons in England and Wales'	Derek Bentley and his execution in 1953

(9 marks)

Note that you have a choice of two individuals. Only write about one. In the exam you must not waste time writing about both of them.

Tip 1: Decode the question

It is very important that you decode the question carefully so that your answer is focused on exactly what the examiner is asking. It is important that you spot

- the focus of the question
- the question type

Tip 2: Stick to the focus of the question

Note that the content focus is on how this person **changed attitudes about punishment**. In this chapter you have explored a great deal about the punishments used in this country. You will know about the rise and fall of the Bloody Code and of punishments like transportation. However, no matter how much you want to show the examiner **all** your other knowledge you must remember one thing: for this question you need to stick to **one individual** and the impact he had on punishment.

Tip 3: Prove that the person was important

Note the question type. You are not being asked to describe what the person did, you are being asked to **explain why he is important**.

Your answer will include examples of what he did, but the main focus must be on:
- how his work or experience affected attitudes to punishment
- how his work or experience fits into the bigger picture of reform (the examiners call this 'context').

Use the model on page 81 to help you do this.

Proving that an individual was important – the keys to success

Show the before as well as the after

Show how Howard's book changed people's understanding of the conditions in gaols. Start with what people actually knew about life in gaols.

Then explain how people's eyes were opened to the terrible conditions as a result of reading the book, and how their attitudes changed. You can use the sentence starters below or invent your own.

Before Howard's book most people did not know much about ...

Howard published his book in 1777. This described scenes such as ...

Howard's book convinced many people that prisons needed improving. The book was a turning point. It meant that for the first time people realised how terrible prison conditions were and how much had to be done.

Show what it led to

Show how Howard's book led to other important developments. Give specific examples to prove your case.

Howard's book was important in the long term because...[over many years it inspired people to improve prisons]

For example in 1783 Sir George Paul was inspired by Howard to build a new model prison. In the 1800s the government was also influenced by his ideas and built ... [describe some of the new ideas used that solved the problems highlighted by Howard]

This meant that prisons ...

Activity

Work in groups. Use the advice provided to answer the practice question below.

Take one event each and produce a draft answer. Then check each other's work carefully.

- Does the answer focus on the question? Remember the questions will ask you to focus on a specific theme.
- Is there a sense of before and after to show the impact the event had on crime and punishment?
- Does the answer **briefly** compare the event to other events that affected this theme?

Provide feedback to each other to improve each draft answer.

Practice questions

The boxes below show two important events. Choose **one** event and explain its importance in changing attitudes to punishments.

Transportation to Australia

The 2005 London bombings

(9 marks)

Section 5: When did policing change the most?

Below you can see PC Ward, whom you met on page 2 of this book. As a serving member of the Metropolitan Police, she is part of a well-trained, well-equipped and well-paid modern police service. She works regular hours, often walks a regular beat and enjoys being part of a very professional force, with a worldwide reputation. But has this always been the case? In this enquiry we will investigate how much policing has changed and, more importantly, decide when it changed the most.

You may already have an idea about when policing changed the most, but as good historians we must look at the evidence in more detail. What sort of changes will we discover – police equipment, the ideas behind the police, the role of police? You may find that some elements of policing have never changed at all – this is continuity! Try to use powerful descriptive adjectives to describe any changes, such as:

fundamental small national local influential unpopular rapid

When you've read this section, you might change your mind completely, or perhaps the evidence will support your original hypothesis.

> First, let me take you back in time and show you how law enforcement and policing has changed. Go back to the **Criminal Moments in Time** on pages 12–17 and pick out any examples you can find of how people caught criminals in the past.

As Britain changed over time, there was certainly a need for law enforcement methods to change. By the late 1700s, ordinary people had begun to form voluntary groups called 'Societies for the Prosecution of Felons'. Some people even set traps around graves to prevent body-snatchers from stealing the bodies of their deceased loved ones!

Policing **did** change – but when did it change the most?

▲ PC Ward, in the uniform of the Metropolitan Police, 2009, just about to start a night shift.

Activities

1 Create your own washing line of policing, similar to the one at the bottom of page 82.

   a) Draw a line along the length of an A3 piece of paper, or alternatively use a piece of string to create your empty washing line.

   b) Write the following dates out on individual sticky notes: 1400s, 1700s, 1800s, 1900s, 2000s. Place these at regular intervals on your washing line.

   c) Look back at the Criminal Moments in Time on pages 12–17. Pick out examples of policing, write these on sticky notes and place them on your washing line in the correct place. An example would be 'Watchmen employed to patrol the streets', and this would be placed on the line between 1700s and 1800s. You may have to move your sticky notes around on the line to fit everything in.

   d) Finally, use your own 'Criminal Moment in Time' for the 21st century and your own knowledge to pick out examples of policing between 1845 and the present day.

2 Look at your completed washing line of policing. When do you think policing might have changed the most? Check back to see if you were right when you have finished this section.

3 What changes to life in Britain do you think affected policing in each period?

4 As you investigate the information and evidence in this section, record the key features of policing in the key features table shown below. Do this for policing in each period of history that you look at: 1450, 1700s, 1800s and 1900s. Think if there are any other details about policing in that time that you can add to your table.

Who collected the evidence?	
Who caught criminals?	
How were they paid?	
How much training was given?	
How did people call for assistance?	
What equipment did they have?	
Did they wear uniform?	

5 Once you have finished your key features table, copy the footsteps below. Make sure you have lots of room to write inside your footprints! Write in the first footprint any examples of **change** that you see when you look at your table. Make sure you remember to include in the second footprint any evidence or information from the pages that you can refer to. In the third footprint, write in any examples of **continuity** that you see. Again, include in the fourth footprint any evidence that you investigate.

6 Once you have come to the end of Section 5, compare your footprints to see where policing has changed the most.

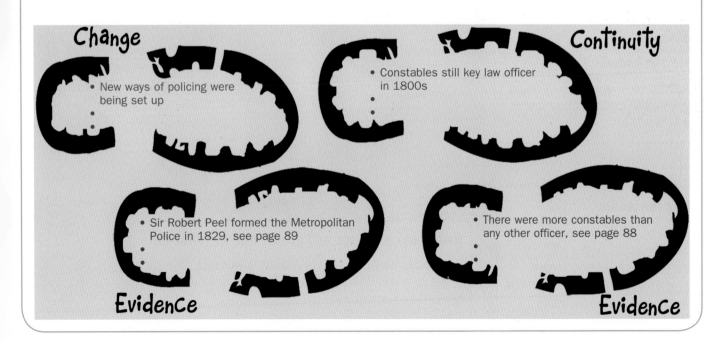

Change
• New ways of policing were being set up

Continuity
• Constables still key law officer in 1800s

Evidence
• Sir Robert Peel formed the Metropolitan Police in 1829, see page 89

Evidence
• There were more constables than any other officer, see page 88

5.1 How effective was policing in 1450?

In 1450 court records from the manor of Wakefield show that Emma Smith of the parish of Kirkburton in Yorkshire was assaulted and injured by the wife of Adam Shepherd of Heppeworth. If this happened today we could simply call the police to help her. But what could she have done over 500 years ago? What methods of law enforcement would Emma Smith be able to use to help get justice?

Visit a constable

From about 1250, constables were the key law enforcement officers in every village or parish, and Emma Smith would want to visit one as soon as possible. This was a voluntary, unpaid job, a duty every male householder was expected to do at some point, for a year at a time. A constable could arrest a criminal. He could also raise the hue and cry.

Raise the hue and cry

Since 1285 if a crime was witnessed then the hue and cry should be raised to summon people to catch a criminal. All able-bodied men hearing the shouts had a duty to join the posse to pursue the criminal.

Did you know?

Hue and cry comes from the Latin hutesium et clamor, which means 'a horn and shouting'.

Ow! I'm hurt and she's getting away! What should I do?

Find the watch

In towns, constables were helped by the watch: citizens who patrolled at night and handed over wrong-doers to the constable in the morning.

Gather her evidence and go and find her attacker

If you had been the victim of a crime it was also your job to get an arrest warrant, find the criminal and bring him/her to the constable.

Call on her tithing group

Tithings were still used – groups of ten men (see page 23). If a member of your tithing broke the law it was your duty to bring him to court or else you would all have to pay compensation to the victim.

1 Which methods would Emma Smith have needed to use to catch her assailant? For each method explain why she would have used it.
2 Overall, what are the strengths and weaknesses of the medieval system?
3 Fill in the key features table (see page 83) to record what you have found out about medieval policing.

Go to the sheriff

Sheriffs were chosen by the monarch and investigated all major crimes, bringing the accused to the Royal Courts. They had the authority to go into any parish they wanted to find criminals – constables could not go beyond their own parish.

If the crime against Emma were serious enough, she could turn to the county sheriff.

Posse Comitatus

The sheriff could summon every male over 15 to catch criminals or stop a riot. This could be a very large number of men!

Manor courts were held by all landowners in their own villages or manors. The landowner was the judge. These courts dealt with workers who had not done enough work on the lord's land or people who had broken other local rules.

What if Emma had been killed?

Coroners

A coroner's duty was to look into any unnatural death on behalf of the King. A local jury would swear an oath on the Bible saying who they thought was guilty of causing the death and the information would be passed to the sheriff.

Summary

The records show that Emma Smith did manage to take the matter to the manor court, and that the wife of Adam Shepherd was fined 12d for the crime.

5.2 Which was greater in the 1700s: change or continuity?

During the 18th century, the population of England and Wales began to increase more quickly, and towns grew in size and number. In 1700, it is estimated that 500,000 people lived in London – this figured doubled over the next 100 years. As the population changed, so did some of the methods of policing but which was greater – change or continuity?

Constables

Constables and watchmen ('Charlies') were still used. They often walked a regular beat, something police still do today. Most constables were still unpaid, and held their office for only a year at a time. However, in some towns a parish tax was raised to pay for them.

Thief-takers

Thief-takers were people who collected rewards for finding and prosecuting criminals. The most famous of these was Jonathan Wild – the 'Thief-taker General', who made a fortune from getting rewards but who also controlled London's criminal gangs. He was eventually hanged in 1725 for receiving stolen goods.

1. Sent to prison in London in 1710

2. Became a city official promising to stop crime – he seemed respectable

3. Organised burglaries then took the rewards for 'finding' the property

4. 1716: Wild arrested lots of criminals who did not obey his orders – he controlled criminal gangs this way

Source 1

A souvenir from Wild's hanging.

5. Finally arrested for receiving stolen goods and hanged in 1725

6. After his death crime went up in London

John and Henry Fielding

The Fielding brothers were two London magistrates who were worried about rising crime and had a number of important ideas for improving law enforcement.

▼ The Fieldings' contribution to policing

1749	They founded the Bow Street Runners, a form of police force. Bow Street was where the Fieldings had their office. The Runners were paid by reward money at first. The government paid for them after 1792. Based in London they would chase criminals across the country if it was needed, and they gave evidence in trials.
1763	The Fieldings set up a Horse Patrol to deal with an increase in highwaymen – at the end of a war lots of ex-soldiers were on the streets and engaged in criminal activities. Money ran out after 18 months and another Horse Patrol did not start up properly until 1805.
1772	The Fieldings began to publish the *Hue & Cry* news-sheet, a listing of crimes and criminals sent across the country and put up in town marketplaces. In the 1800s this became the *Police Gazette*, published to inform the public of crimes and to offer rewards for information. Other countries copied this idea, including Australia. By 1914 it was published daily.

Other methods

Thames River Police

In 1798 the Thames River Police was set up to stop thefts from boats on the River Thames. Two magistrates called John Harriott and Patrick Colquhoun, inspired by the Fielding brothers, convinced ship owners to pay the initial costs, and at first there were 50 officers. In their first year alone they recovered £122,000 worth of property from criminals, including a great deal of stolen coal. As a result of this success, in 1800 the government began funding the River Police.

Activity

Look at the information about policing in the 1700s. Fill in the key features table from page 83 and use your footsteps to record changes and continuity. Remember that when making notes you should use your own words. If you include a quotation it must be the exact words, and include the provenance – who said it and when.

The army

The army was the final method of law enforcement. It was often used to stop protests, after the Riot Act was first read out aloud.

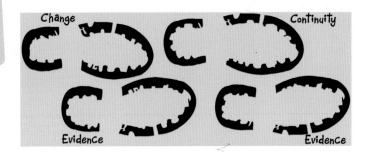

5.3 Which was greater in the 1800s: change or continuity?

In the early 1800s the population began to increase rapidly, and the old system struggled to keep up with enforcing the law, especially in large towns and cities. How much did policing change?

Source 1 shows the number of people required to police just one London parish in 1811. A beadle, for example, was employed to round up beggars and take them to workhouses. A scavenger collected up rubbish – most of which was recycled.

Activity

How many constables can you count in Source 1? What does that suggest about crime in this part of London in 1811? What else can you learn from this source?

Source 1

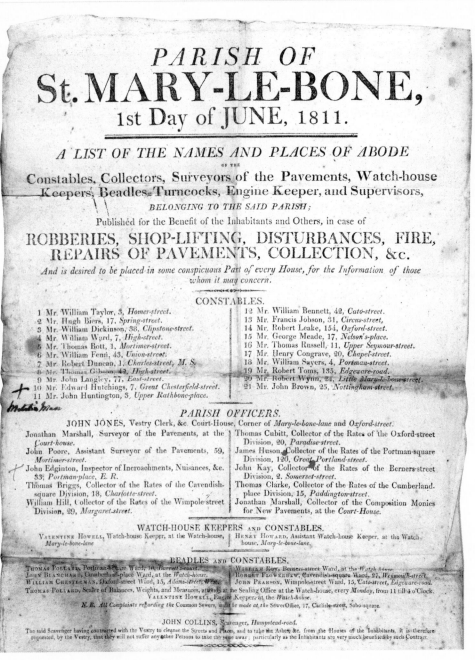

◀ A list of constables and other parish officers for the wealthy parish of St Mary-Le-Bone, London, 1811.

Innovations?

During the 19th century policing seems to have fundamentally changed, thanks to the famous reforms of Sir Robert Peel, the Home Secretary who set up the Metropolitan Police Force.

However, was it as straightforward as it seems?

Activity

As you research the 1800s, fill in your key features table from page 83 and use your footprints again to look for both changes and continuity. Perhaps some 'new' ideas were simply extending ideas from the previous century?

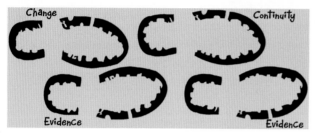

Change   Continuity

Evidence   Evidence

Source 2

▲ Sir Robert Peel, the politician who had the skills to set up the police force. This is why police were often called Bobbies or Peelers.

1800 City of Glasgow Police formed, funded by a tax, to patrol, investigate, and arrest criminals in Glasgow.

1800 Thames River Police fully funded by government.

1805 Horse Patrol revived in Bow Street. They had blue jackets, red waistcoats and wore top hats. Their nickname was 'Robin Redbreasts' and they were armed with a pistol, a sword and a truncheon.

1829 Sir Robert Peel formed the Metropolitan Police in London. These were 3,200 professional policemen whose job it was to patrol, investigate, and arrest criminals across all of London, gathering evidence to bring about prosecutions. The force was paid for by the government and was based at Scotland Yard.

POLICE: 1800s

1842 The Metropolitan Police set up the first detective force. Plain-clothes officers were frequently used.

1856 It was compulsory for towns and counties to set up police forces.

1830 148,000 copies of the *Police Gazette* newspaper distributed at a cost of £1,365.

1835 Towns other than London could set up their own police forces.

1884 39,000 police officers working in Britain.

1800s: the role of the police

You have seen that new ideas were introduced – but what was it actually like to be a Peeler in the 1800s?

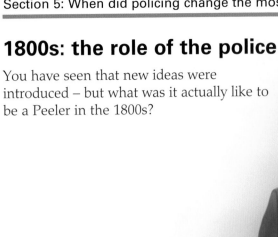

Number: identifying number on collar so the constable could be held accountable by the public.

Equipment: wooden truncheon, handcuffs, wooden rattle.

Uniform: blue, including top hat – designed to be unlike the army. Police helmets were introduced in 1870. The collar was strengthened to prevent strangulation.

Age: under 35
Height: 5ft 7in minimum

Hours: 12 hours a day, six days a week.

Salary: One guinea (£1.05) a week.

◀ Police Constable in the Metropolitan Police, 1829

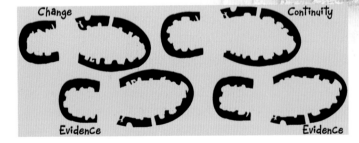

Activity

Have a look at the sources and information on pages 90–91 to find out more. Pick out the key points of the role of police constables, fill in your key features table from page 83 and again use your footsteps to pick up changes and continuity.

Source 1

Written by Sir Richard Mayne in 1829. Mayne was the first commissioner in charge of the police, staying in the job for 39 years. After 1850 crime began to fall – had the presence of uniformed police constables on the streets been able to prevent crime?

The primary object of an efficient police is the prevention of crime: the next that of detection and punishment of offenders if crime is committed. To these ends all the efforts of police must be directed. The protection of life and property, the preservation of public tranquillity, and the absence of crime, will alone prove whether those efforts have been successful and whether the objects for which the police were appointed have been attained.

Source 2

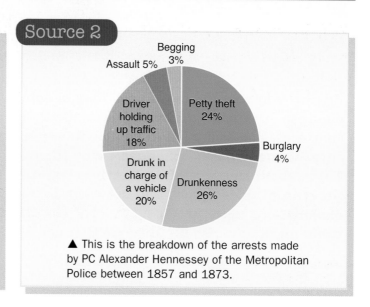

▲ This is the breakdown of the arrests made by PC Alexander Hennessey of the Metropolitan Police between 1857 and 1873.

Source 3

▲ In 1891 a patent was issued in Glasgow for the first police signal box. Constables could now contact the stations while on their beat.

Source 4

▲ A drawing of the police stopping a Chartist protest in the 1830s. This was made for a book published in 1886. Police were now used to deal with protests and unrest not the army. Metropolitan Police officers could find themselves used elsewhere in the country. For example in 1837 a sergeant and 11 constables were sent from London to Huddersfield to stop protests during an election.

- Ever since Roman times the victims of crime had had to gather their own evidence for prosecutions. Now the police were paid to do just this – a big burden had been lifted.
- There was strict discipline in the police, perhaps because of drunkenness – the cause of 80 per cent of all dismissals. The police punishment book shows that the first policeman taken on, and given the number 1, was sacked for being drunken after only four hours on the job!
- Pay was quite poor – policemen earned less than a skilled labourer did. However, people still complained about paying the local tax that funded them.

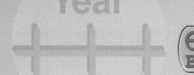

By now you should have a good idea of some of the changes in policing that went on in the 18th and 19th centuries. You will need to be able to **explain** the **significance** of these changes – why they were important. Think about the powerful adjectives (right) mentioned at the start of the enquiry, and use them to make your explanations more **precise**. ('Precise' is a word used in exam mark schemes for answers that get A and A*!)

Adjectives

fundamental   small

national   local

influential

unpopular   rapid

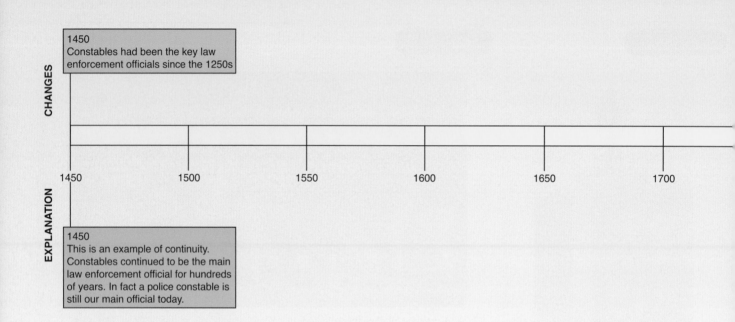

CHANGES

1450
Constables had been the key law enforcement officials since the 1250s

| 1450 | 1500 | 1550 | 1600 | 1650 | 1700 |

EXPLANATION

1450
This is an example of continuity. Constables continued to be the main law enforcement official for hundreds of years. In fact a police constable is still our main official today.

Don't worry if you find there are periods of very little change. Decades or centuries of continuity are always there in History and show stability – their importance is just as significant as any changes. By the time we came along though, there was plenty that needed to be done!

Henry Fielding   John Fielding

Activities

Above the timeline are some of the changes you have studied. There are plenty more you could add. Below the timeline is where you can add explanations about the significance of the changes. Some have been started for you – others you will have to write yourself.

1 Copy the timeline. Complete the explanations for each of the changes to policing on the timeline. Can you use any of these powerful adjectives?

| fundamental | small | national | local |
| influential | unpopular | rapid | |

2 Look back at your footsteps and the previous pages to add three more changes – the ones you think are really significant.

3 Add explanations for the three changes you have added.

4 Extend your explanations by using connectives such as 'Without this change ... ', 'As a result of this change ... ' and 'However ... '

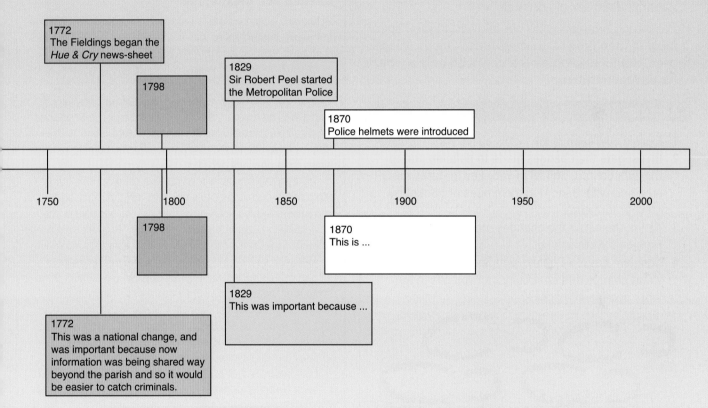

1772
The Fieldings began the *Hue & Cry* news-sheet

1798

1829
Sir Robert Peel started the Metropolitan Police

1870
Police helmets were introduced

1750   1800   1850   1900   1950   2000

1798

1870
This is ...

1829
This was important because ...

1772
This was a national change, and was important because now information was being shared way beyond the parish and so it would be easier to catch criminals.

You have now worked well on an important exam skill. Share your work and compare it to others in your class:

- What have they done well?
- How could they improve their explanations?
- What ideas will you use in your own answers next time?

Remember – here you have revised changes **before** the 20th century. After you study the changes that took place **during** the 20th century, come back to your timeline and add more changes and explanations – there is plenty of space waiting for you to fill!

5.4 Which was greater in the 1900s: change or continuity?

What were the changes to policing in the 20th century?

By 1900 policing had changed a great deal – but it was still not perfect. Some of the key problems were:

- There were 200 different local police forces, each with its own way of doing things. Communication between them was poor.
- Pay and training were poor. The only training a new recruit got was some basic military drill.
- Record-keeping was poor, and there was no national database of criminals.
- Policemen (women were not allowed to join) spent most of their time on their own walking their local beat – up to 30 kilometres a day, with only a whistle for communication.

Activities

1. Explain why each of the points above was a problem.
2. Investigate the changes made to policing during the 20th century and fill in your key features table (see page 83). Record any changes or continuity on your footsteps.
3. As you research the changes, decide how far the problems were solved.
4. Compare Source 1 below with Source 2 on page 91. What change and continuity can you see in the work done by the police?

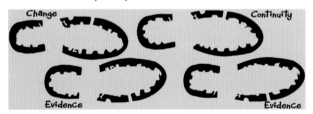

(see page 83)
Source 2 on page 91.

Source 1

Drunk and disorderly	35%	
Drunk	25%	
Stealing a car	16%	
Disorderly behaviour	8%	
Vandalism	6%	
Drunk driving	5%	
Soliciting (by prostitutes)	3%	
Possessing drugs	2%	

◀ Minor crimes dealt with by Birmingham police in 1996.

Training and recruitment

To recruit the best quality constables, police pay is now good. Women can now be police officers. The police also try to attract recruits who reflect the diversity of the population they serve.

A National Police Training College started in 1947 and all constables have at least 14 weeks of basic training before starting work. Specialist training continues according to local need, or career development – for example in Road Policing Units.

Science and technology

Technology advanced greatly in the 20th century. In 1901 the first police photographer was employed, and in 1937 the 999 emergency number was introduced.

In 1902 fingerprints were used successfully to prosecute a criminal for the first time – a certain Harry Jackson, for burglary. Around this time the existence of different blood groups was discovered, which allowed the police to analyse blood samples and eliminate suspects. More recently DNA samples have been used as evidence – even helping to solve crimes from previous decades.

The police experimented with mobile radio in 1923, fitting morse code transmitters into police cars and telephone boxes soon after; now all officers are issued with mobile phones that use a special system to keep communication constant even during disasters, for example during the July 2005 bombings in London.

Many police cars have advanced computer technology built into them, for example automatic vehicle number plate recognition systems, as well as cameras to record drivers' behaviour and check car speeds. Camera technology is also built into police helicopters, providing night vision when pursuing criminals in the dark. Evidence from security cameras has also helped the police solve crimes.

Computers also allow for improved record keeping. There is now a National Criminal Record, which all forces can use, with databases ranging from fingerprints and DNA to missing persons. Police can also share information on the internet – for example, wanted criminal websites, which work hand-in-hand with TV programmes like *Crimestoppers*.

Police Community Support Officers (PCSOs)

There are now Police Community Support Officers, introduced in 2002, who support the work of the police. They are not as well trained as full officers, have a modified uniform and carry less equipment. Their main job is to provide a visible presence in communities, tackle anti-social behaviour and gather evidence when dealing with minor incidents.

Role

The role of the police has not changed – dealing with minor and major crimes, maintaining public order and even giving directions. However, within the police there are now many highly skilled, specialist groups that focus on particular problems. These include the Homicide and Serious Crime Unit, the Counter Terrorism Command (also called SO15) and Forensic Services.

Equipment

Ordinary police are still unarmed – although until 1936 they could arm themselves if they wanted to. This reassures the public and stops criminals from automatically arming themselves too. Specialist officers do carry weapons: SO19 is the specialist firearms branch of the police and in 1991 'Armed Response Vehicles' were first introduced to the streets of London.

Most police now wear body armour to protect themselves. They also carry a new sort of truncheon, and can be authorised to carry electric Tasers that stun criminals. Special riot gear is used sometimes, as are weapons such as CS gas, which can cause temporary blindness.

Organisation

There are now only 43 different police forces in England and Wales, with a total of 141,354 police officers (September 2006 figures). The forces work in similar ways and collaborate effectively. They are co-ordinated by the Association of Chief Police Officers, formed in 1948.

Some people want a single national police force – but others think this could put too much power in the hands of government, similar fears that people had in the early 1800s!

Police powers

Police powers have changed a little.

Arrest: Police have the right to arrest someone they suspect is committing an offence. This is a common law power we all have too!

Search: The police normally need a warrant to search a property – though not if a breach of the peace is occurring. A warrant is given by a magistrate who must agree the search is reasonable.

Detention: The police can hold a suspect for up to 24 hours before charging or releasing them. They can apply for an extension to this, for up to 96 hours. For terrorist offences it can be extended to 28 days.

Fines: Police cannot arrest people for minor offences like speeding, but they can issue on-the-spot fines.

Transport

Over the century cars and motorbikes improved police speed and effectiveness, although criminals also benefited from improved transport. In the 1970s the police moved from having the local 'bobby on the beat' to fast response car units that could rush to the scene of a crime. However most forces have now re-introduced foot patrols, as the public find it reassuring to see police officers on their streets.

The police also use helicopters, horses, mountain bikes, boats and some light aircraft if they are required.

Source 2

▲ A woman police officer on traffic duty in 1964. In 1914 when World War I broke out, Nina Boyle, an ex-Suffragette, formed the Women Police Volunteers. It was not until 1973 that women were fully integrated into the police service.

Activity

Match Sources 2–5 to the changes on pages 94–95.

Source 3

▲ A Police Community Support Officer.

Source 4

▲ 1923 saw the first experiments with mobile radio for constables. These are 'Crossley Tenders' – vans fitted with wireless telegraphy – at the Derby.

Source 5

◄ Police in riot gear confront protestors near Downing Street, 1997.

Activities

You have now looked at all the information and evidence to do with policing – and seen many changes, along with some continuity. Before we look at an exam question, you should spend some time thinking about the whole theme of policing and what the evidence tells you. Look back at all the information you have recorded on your footsteps about change and continuity.

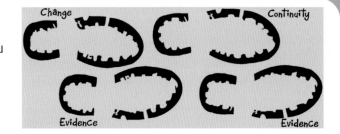

1 For each of these statements, decide how far you agree with it using the scale below. Be ready to provide the reasons and evidence to support your decision.

- Some elements of policing have not changed much at all.
- The police force changed most significantly in the 18th century.
- The police force changed most significantly in the 19th century.
- The police force changed most dramatically in the 20th century.
- The Fielding brothers had the most important ideas about policing.
- Peel had the most important ideas about policing.
- There are many influential people who changed policing.

```
Disagree                                    Agree
    1       2       3       4       5
◄──────────────────────────────────────►
```

2 Discuss your decisions with your learning partner. Can they explain any differences they have compared to your decisions? What reasons and evidence do they give for this? Does it make you change your mind?

3 Repeat questions 1 and 2 with two statements of your own.

Factors affecting policing

You have seen **how** policing changed from the 17th to the 20th century, but can you also explain **why** it changed when it did?

To do this you need to look at the attitudes, approaches and concerns people had during this whole period. Organising and discussing the information in different ways helps you to develop your explanations. It will help you to understand why there were changes at certain times and not others. It will also help you to understand the continuity, or lack of change over some periods.

Concept map A

Key

| | 1500s–1700s | | 1700s–1800s | | 1800s–1900s | | 1900s–present day |

Population
In the 16th and 17th centuries, the majority of the population lived in villages, where the traditional system of constables was still used effectively. The population was growing slowly and reached only 5 million people in 1700.

Invasion of privacy
In the 1700s many people felt that a police force would be used to spy on citizens and be used by the government to place limits on freedom. A police force was seen as a continental idea used by European despots.

The Fieldings
In the mid-1700s the Fielding brothers had many innovative ideas about law enforcement. They were convinced society had changed and the old systems no longer worked. They had a passion to make changes happen, and were able to convince law makers to fund some of them.

Cost
In the 1700s governments did not have a tradition of getting closely involved in the running of law enforcement or indeed many other aspects of society. They did not have the income from taxes to pay for big reforms either, except during wars.

Fear of protest
After the French Revolution in 1789, law makers were scared of any protest that might spark a similar revolution in Britain, and they thought a police force might be helpful to stop this. There were many protests in the years after 1815, often about food prices, changes to jobs and the right to vote.

Government and taxation
In the 1800s governments began to become more involved in managing society in Britain. A long war with France (which ended in 1815) had got people used to paying higher local and national taxes, so the government could afford expensive reforms and policies such as funding the police.

Success
The success of the Bow Street Runners and Thames River Police convinced many people a professional police force would be an excellent idea.

Failure
Many people did not think that a police force would be a success. Even after it had been formed some people were critical – as late as 1868 *Fun* magazine called the police 'an organised bunch of ruffians'.

Peel
Sir Robert Peel was a politician determined to reform law enforcement when he was Home Secretary in the 1820s. He had the personality and the influential position to be able to bring in his changes.

Fear of crime

There was a widespread fear that crime was increasing rapidly, especially violent crime. Statistics suggest this was actually true following the end of the French wars. A solution to this problem was needed.

Urbanisation

From the 1750s, and especially after 1800, the growth of towns and cities meant that the old system of constables seemed unable to deal adequately with the problems of crime any more – criminals could simply vanish into the busy streets. This was particularly the case in London, where the laws were made and many law makers lived.

Population

Britain's population increased rapidly after 1800. It went from 8 million people in 1801 to over 40 million in 1901. This swift change caused fear of crime to increase.

Fear of crime

In 1997 32 per cent of people said they felt unsafe walking out at night. Newspapers and TV stories about crime contribute to this fear. After the July 2005 bombings in London, fear of crime, particularly terrorism, increased and the police were given increased powers to detain suspects and to carry weapons.

Satisfaction

In the 20th century most people were satisfied with the modern police service, and dramatic change was not seen as necessary.

Technology

As technology developed the police were able to have increasingly sophisticated equipment.

Concept map B

Another approach is to look at the **factors** from page 7 again, and build a different sort of concept map. Instead of thinking about why there **were** changes in the 19th or 20th centuries, think about why policing **didn't** change much in the 18th century.

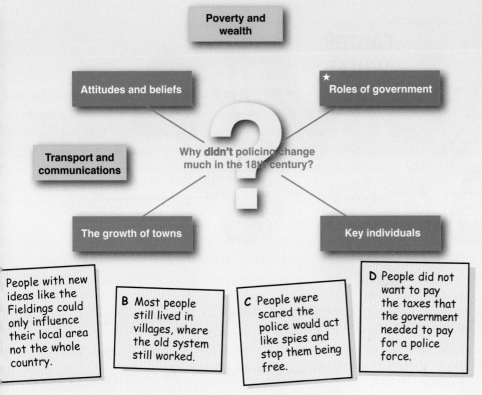

You could try this with other questions. For example:
- Why did policing change in the 19th century?
- Why did policing change in the 20th century?

Activities

We have built up this concept map for you. It explains why policing was slow to change. It's almost finished. All you have to do is copy it and finish it off.

1 The factors in red boxes and linked to the question with red lines were important in holding back change. The pink cards A–D provide evidence of this. On your own version of the map write or place the pink cards in the correct place on the red lines.

2 Look back at the information in Concept map A. Can you link any of the factors in the gold boxes to the question, based on what the information tells you? Use a different coloured card to provide evidence of your own ideas.

3 The star shows which factor we think was the most important in holding back change in policing. Do you agree? Why?

Section 6: Why have attitudes to crime changed?

This extension unit asks you to think carefully about why attitudes to crime have changed. You will need to be able to do two things.

1 **Describe** the difference between attitudes in the two periods of time or between different people in society.

2 **Explain** why attitudes changed. For this you will need to think about the factors you have used earlier in your course.

The three topics you will investigate are very different, and come from very different time periods, see page 101. However, the focus for your thinking will remain the same – **how** and **why** attitudes have changed. To get top marks the examiner will be looking for you to show:

How a range of factors led to changed attitudes and changed treatment of people.

How the factors link to each other.

Witchcraft in the 17th century

▲ This woodcut shows three witches being tortured in front of King James I – who was king of Scotland and England at the turn of the 17th century. He believed in witches and wrote a book about them in which he said that 'these detestable slaves of the devil, the witches ... [deserve] most severely to be punished'.

Conscientious objectors in the two world wars

Women and the law in the 20th century

▲ This is Mary Barbour wearing her robes of office as a councillor in the 1920s in Glasgow. She was the first woman Labour councillor in Glasgow, and ended up running committees and serving as a magistrate. Attitudes to women changed greatly during her lifetime and Mary played her part in this. She was involved in running a campaign for fair rents; she helped to set up a family planning clinic; she became a magistrate; and she was always trying to improve the welfare of women and children.

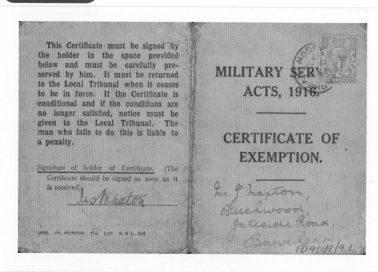

◀ James Maxton was conscripted to the army in 1916. He claimed exemption from military service on the grounds of conscientious objection. He was sent to prison for helping to organise strikes before his Military Tribunal could be finished, and then in 1917 he was released and agreed to work for a firm of canal barge builders. This is his certificate of exemption. In 1922 he became an MP.

6.1 How do changing attitudes explain the rise and fall of witchcraft?

In the 16th and 17th centuries, around 1,000 people in England and Wales were executed for the crime of witchcraft. When and why did attitudes to witchcraft change?

Activity

Pages 102–105 show you a range of evidence and information about witchcraft. Create a revision booklet to use when you are close to the exam. Remember to use details from the witchcraft cases to support any points you make.

Complete your booklet using the following headings:

1 **The rise and fall of witchcraft**
   - When did witchcraft trials increase?
   - When did witchcraft trials die out?

2 **A typical witchcraft trial**
   - What can you learn about a typical witchcraft case?
   - Which cases agree with the typical case on page 105?
   - Which ones show untypical features?

3 **Changing attitudes**
   - What influenced attitudes in the 1500s?
   - When and why did attitudes change? Look at cases from the 1660s onwards to find evidence.
   - What do you think was the most important factor in these changing attitudes?

4 **Fear of crime**
   - Many pamphlets were sold telling gruesome stories about these cases. How might this have affected fear of crime?

Until 1542 witchcraft had always been a church matter, but around the same time that Henry VIII made England Protestant he also made witchcraft a crime.

Witchcraft trials would seem like normal trials. The accusers would present their charge and witnesses would appear. However 90 per cent of those accused were elderly women, with no one to speak for them in court. Only rarely was torture used. The witch hunts led by Matthew Hopkins in 1645 were an exception – he used humiliation and sleep deprivation to get 'confessions' from the 36 women he accused. A witch would normally be hanged only if she had used her powers to kill or to damage property. Nineteen of the suspects accused by Hopkins were hanged.

Source 1

▲ A woodcut showing a village 'swimming a witch'. It was believed the innocent would sink. If they floated then it was evidence they were guilty and would be checked for Devil's marks, the final proof of witchcraft.

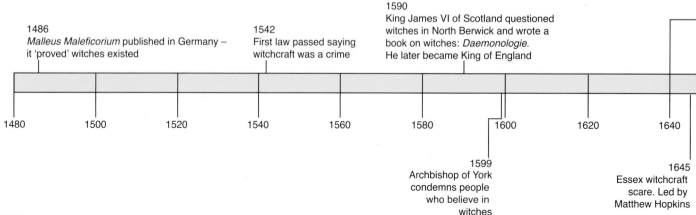

1486
Malleus Maleficorium published in Germany – it 'proved' witches existed

1542
First law passed saying witchcraft was a crime

1590
King James VI of Scotland questioned witches in North Berwick and wrote a book on witches: *Daemonologie.* He later became King of England

1599
Archbishop of York condemns people who believe in witches

1645
Essex witchcraft scare. Led by Matthew Hopkins

The rise and fall of witchcraft between 1450 and 1750

Factors	Rise	Fall
Religion	New extreme Protestant beliefs said the Devil was always trying to lead Christians away from God. People had no explanations for illness and disease – they thought God or the Devil was involved.	As beliefs became less extreme the numbers of accusations declined. Science increasingly provided explanations for disease. The concept of chance was also becoming more influential.
Governments	The governments during the Civil War were very religious, especially the Puritans who ran the English Republic.	After the restoration of the monarchy, governments were more secular – Charles II even set up the Royal Society to further scientific knowledge. Governments no longer needed to prove their godliness by prosecuting witches.
Attitudes and beliefs	As society changed people trusted each other less, and were worried about different ways of thinking and behaving. This was especially true during the Civil War in the 1640s. There was tension in communities when the rich clamped down on the poor with various laws (as you have already seen in Section 3).	Society settled down once peace returned and life returned to normal in the later 1600s. The end of the Civil War saw the end of the witch craze. Society changed so that there were fewer personal links within villages. The rich were increasingly educated and separate from the poor.
Poverty	The first half of the 17th century saw wages and work decline. This led to tension and bad feelings in communities – most accusations of witchcraft were against the poor.	Economic conditions changed and tensions reduced in villages and towns.

Source 2

County	Accusations 1560–1700	Executions 1560–1700
Sussex	33	1
Surrey	71	5
Hertfordshire	81	8
Kent	132	16
Essex	473	82
Total	**790**	**112**

▲ Accusations compared to executions: data from the south-east of England. The peak years for accusations were 1558–1603. Many accusations did not make it to court.

Source 3

Extracts from Thomas Hobbes' book *Leviathan*, published in 1651. 'Rude' meant uneducated. Hobbes was part of the Enlightenment movement.

> From this ignorance of how to distinguish dreams and such fancies from vision and sense did arise the greatest part of the religion in times past ... nowadays [this ignorance causes] the opinion that rude people have of fairies, ghosts, and goblins, and of the power of witches.

Source 4

This is from the *Spectator* magazine in 1714, when Jane Wenham was on trial. The writer was trying to show that he did not believe in witchcraft.

> She goes by the Name of *Moll White*, and has made the Country ring with several imaginary Exploits which are palmed upon her. If the Dairy Maid does not make her Butter come so soon as she should have it, *Moll White* is at the Bottom of the Churn. If a Horse sweats in the Stable, *Moll White* has been upon his Back. If a Hare makes an unexpected escape from the Hounds, the Huntsman curses *Moll White*... notice a Tabby Cat that sat in the Chimney-Corner ... *Moll* is said often to turn into the same shape, the Cat is reported to have spoken twice or thrice in her Life, and to have played several Pranks above the Capacity of an ordinary Cat.

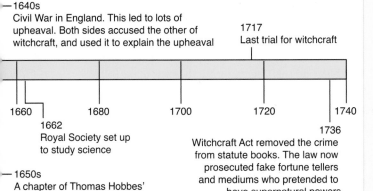

—1640s
Civil War in England. This led to lots of upheaval. Both sides accused the other of witchcraft, and used it to explain the upheaval

1717
Last trial for witchcraft

1660 — 1680 — 1700 — 1720 — 1740

1662
Royal Society set up to study science

1736
Witchcraft Act removed the crime from statute books. The law now prosecuted fake fortune tellers and mediums who pretended to have supernatural powers

—1650s
A chapter of Thomas Hobbes' book *Leviathan* disproves witchcraft

Investigating witchcraft cases

These pages have information from real trials that will help you to complete your revision booklet. Think carefully about the attitudes that lie behind the accusations and also the verdicts. You can do further research using the Scottish Witchcraft online database at www.shc.ed.ac.uk/research/witches.

1570 Richard and Clemence Marshall, of Croydon, were found guilty of bewitching the horses and cows of three different men. The judge calculated the cost of each animal during the trial.

Accusations that came to trial usually had to come from more than one person. Accusations from neighbours often centred around disputes and quarrels.

1593 Alice Samuel, 76, her husband and daughter were accused of making a ten-year-old girl fall sick. The girl's sisters also claimed to have been bewitched. When Alice denied the charge the girls had fits, but recovered when she admitted it. Alice and her family were executed.

1660s Alice Huson and Doll Bilby were accused by a girl of bewitching her. The girl's parents did not believe her and sent for three doctors. The girl went to a relative's house to recover. After four years she still insisted she was bewitched, and the parents accused Alice and Doll of the crime. They were found guilty.

1682 Temperance Lloyd was hanged for being a witch during a time of local food shortages. During her trial she claimed the Devil had met her in the street, that she had turned into a cat and also that she had sneaked a doll into a woman's bedchamber.

1683 Jane Dodson was on trial for witchcraft at the Old Bailey. She was acquitted as there was no evidence of her crime, and she had character witnesses to speak for her.

Source 1

A Treatise of Witchcraft.

Wherein sundry Propositions are laid downe, plainely discouering the wickednesse of that damnable Art, with diuerse other speciall points annexed, not impertinent to the same, such as ought diligently of euery Christian to be considered.

With a true Narration of the Witch-crafts which *Mary Smith*, wife of *Henry Smith Glouer*, did practise: Of her contract vocally made between the Deuill and her, in solemne termes, by whose meanes she hurt sundry persons whom she enuied: Which is confirmed by her owne confession, and also from the publique Records of the Examination of diuerse vpon their oathes: And lastly, of her death and execution, for the same; which was on the twelfth day of Ianua-rie last past.

By ALEXANDER ROBERTS B.D. and Preacher of Gods Word at *Kings-Linne* in *Norffolke*.

EXOD. 22.18.
Thou shalt not suffer a Witch to liue.

Impium est a nos illis esse Remissos, quos cœlestis Pietas, Non Patitur impunitos: Alarus Rex apud Cassiodorum.

LONDON,

Printed by N. O. for SAMVEL MAN, and are to be sold at his Shop in Pauls Church-yard at the signe of the Ball.
1 6 1 6.

▲ A pamphlet from 1616. How many references to God and religion can you find? The pamphlet was even sold next to St Paul's cathedral in London!

A typical case

1 A villager, usually an old widow, asks for help from a better-off neighbour, but is refused. Often this followed years of suspicion and tension between the widow and the neighbour.

2 The widow walks away, muttering and cursing quietly, maybe even uttering a threat. Both feel angry. The neighbour feels guilty.

3 Some time afterwards, something terrible happens to the neighbour or her family – an illness in her children or animals, perhaps even a death.

> **1699** Mary Poole was on trial at the Old Bailey, having 'juggled' a victim out of some money and spoken in a strange 'canting dialect'. One of the witnesses accused her of witchcraft. She was found guilty of theft, and branded.

> I suspect witchcraft – what else could have caused this sudden illness?

> If she is a witch, we must stop her before she can do any more harm.

4 The neighbour looks for an explanation of this terrible event. She knows the widow's reputation as a strange woman and the rumours that she is a witch. She suspects this event could be a witch's evil work.

5 She mentions her thoughts to friends who tell her about other examples of things that have gone wrong when they refused to help the widow. They decide to accuse the widow before any more harm is done.

> **1712** Jane Wenham went on trial for cursing a neighbour's animals. She was found guilty by the jury but the judge did not execute her. Instead he asked the Queen for a royal pardon. She was then looked after by the aristocrat Earl Cowper, who gave her a house on his country estate.

> **1716** Mary Hickes and her daughter were executed for witchcraft after removing their stockings to summon a rainstorm.

> **1724** Coustantine Mac-yennis was accused of murder. Witnesses said he claimed he had killed a witch, and that he believed his laundry woman was a witch. By the 1720s this belief was enough proof for him to be locked up as a 'lunatick'.

Source 2

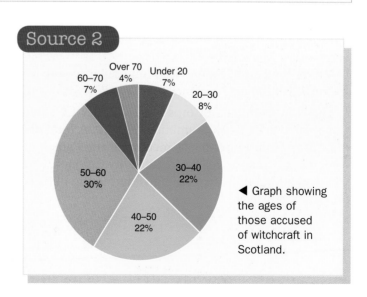

Over 70 4%
Under 20 7%
60–70 7%
20–30 8%
30–40 22%
50–60 30%
40–50 22%

◀ Graph showing the ages of those accused of witchcraft in Scotland.

6.2 'Conchies': 'slackers' or an important freedom?

In the First and Second World Wars conscription was introduced: young men had to join the army and fight for their country. However, in both wars some people refused to fight. These people were called conscientious objectors (COs), or 'conchies'.

But how did people react to COs, and was there any change in how they were treated between the two wars?

Quakers and some other religious groups believed that fighting was against their religion.

Religious beliefs

Political beliefs

Some socialists believed that the German people were not Britons' enemy.

Why did people become conscientious objectors?

Many people thought COs were simply cowards.

Cowardice?

Moral beliefs

Some people believed that war was morally wrong.

When conscription was introduced in the First World War, the government included an option for people to apply for 'exemption from military duty' because of their beliefs. Many 'alternativist' COs 'did their bit' through war work other than fighting and some won medals for their bravery as stretcher-bearers or as ambulance drivers at the front. COs who refused – around 6,000 'absolutists' – were sent to prison to do hard labour as punishment.

In 1916 a Home Office Scheme changed conditions – absolutists could now agree to work in camps set up at prisons like Dartmoor or Wakefield. Those who still refused to work stayed in prison; however they had to serve less solitary confinement than originally sentenced, and did not have to wear the arrow uniform of criminals. They did still have to do hard labour and remain silent except when exercising.

When war ended in 1918 COs were banned from voting for five years but this did not include anyone who had done war-related work like driving ambulances or clearing mines. This measure was not repeated in the Second World War, another war about freedom. By then attitudes had changed quite a lot, especially after COs had been seen to do useful work.

Tribunals were run by civilians not military men. Prison was only used if no other work could be found. Around 29,000 COs worked in farming or factories. Many COs still saw their jobs as 'their bit' for the war effort. However they often experienced unpopularity and accusations of cowardice and over 70 councils sacked COs who were working for them.

The Non-Combatant Corps was set up for COs who chose to help with war-related activities like ambulance work. A total of 6,766 men served in the Corps, including some as medics for the Parachute Regiment. They were described as 'excellent in battle' by Colonel A. Young. A further 465 worked in bomb disposal units during the Blitz. None could be promoted however.

Source 1

Clause 8, Representation of the People Act, 1918.

Any person who has been exempted from all military service on the ground of conscientious objections ... shall be disqualified from registering or voting at a parliamentary or local election.

Source 2

Results from CO tribunals 1939–41.

63 per cent exempted from military duty did civilian work
20 per cent agreed to non-military jobs in the army
17 per cent ordered to join the army

Source 3

Lieutenant General Sir N Crookenden, describing the 1944 D-Day landing hospitals set up by the Parachute Field Ambulance unit.

Many of these men were conscientious objectors ... who refused to bear arms but were quite willing to jump or glide into action as medical orderlies. Their levels of education, courage and skill were exceptional.

Number of COs	
World War I	16,000
World War II	59,192

Activities

1 Work in pairs. Read the sources and information on pages 106–109 and put together a presentation – it could be a presentation given to your class, a slideshow or a podcast. You should explain:
   • how COs were treated in each war
   • what the attitudes to the COs were in each war – look at the attitudes of government and the attitudes of ordinary people.
   • how attitudes changed between the wars.
2 Overall why do you think attitudes to the COs changed?

World War I

Source 4

10 May 1916, a debate in Parliament by MPs.

Sir William Byles 'asked whether Mr Rendel Wyatt, a young schoolmaster in a Quaker school, a conscientious objector under the Military Service Act, has been arrested and imprisoned, and made to scrub floors and carry coal for fourteen or fifteen hours a day; whether he has since been given a month on bread and water and put in irons for refusing to drill; whether he is now in a dark cell with twelve others.'

Mr Snowden said 'Cannot the right honourable gentleman see that the best way to avoid all trouble is to put a stop to the practice at once by making an example of the men who are guilty of this torture?'

Mr Tennant: 'I am asking the House not to believe all this tittle-tattle.'

Source 5

James Lovegrove was 16 when this happened in 1916.

On my way to work one morning a group of women surrounded me. They started shouting and yelling at me, calling me all sorts of names for not being a soldier! Do you know what they did? They stuck a white feather in my coat, meaning I was a coward. Oh, I did feel dreadful, so ashamed.

Source 6

◄ COs in the First World War doing hard labour at Dartmoor Prison. In 1917 all prisoners were removed from Dartmoor Prison and 1,100 COs were sent there. Conditions were more relaxed than in other prisons, leading to newspaper headlines such as 'The Coddled Conscience Men' and 'Pampered Pets'. Seventy-three COs died in prison during World War I.

Source 7

Fenner Brockway, a CO in the First World War, said this about COs in both wars.

The conscientious objector has stood for eternally desirable values when they were threatened with suppression, and the world is a less evil place because they have done so...[but] the conscientious objector has no right to reject war in the present unless he spends his life in helping to make a future without war.

Source 8

▲ A cartoon from the *Daily Mirror* in 1915 entitled 'The Slacker's excuse for not joining'.

Does this attitude contrast with that of the MPs in Source 4 (page 107)? Do you think the newspaper would have shown the same attitude in the Second World War? Which evidence on page 109 suggests COs were more accepted by the Second World War?

World War II

Source 9

▲ A newspaper cartoon from 1939 with the heading 'Conscientious Objector: I don't want to fight anybody, but I don't mind joining up for the duration of the lull.'

How much had attitudes to COs changed in the newspapers?

Source 10

The British Prime Minister, Neville Chamberlain, 1939.

We learned something about this in the Great War, and I think we found that it was both a useless and an exasperating waste of time and effort to attempt to force such people to act in a manner which was contrary to their principles.

Source 11

Bernard Hicken was a CO from Yorkshire in the Second World War. He was allowed to work in farming instead of fighting. He then volunteered for medical trials to find a cure for scabies, which was a problem for soldiers, and went on starvation diet experiments.

I thought this was something I'd like to do. It's humanitarian, it's helping people, and also there's a certain amount of risk. It was an opportunity to do my bit in a more positive way.

Meet the Examiner: Analysing and evaluating change

You will have two questions on your extension unit. Part (a) is worth 9 marks.

It could ask you to:

- identify key features of a crime, punishment or period
- give reasons for a crime, punishment or development
- describe change and continuity within or between periods.

The second question, part (b), worth 16 marks, requires a longer answer. You may be asked to analyse and evaluate how an aspect of crime and punishment changed over time. This Exam Buster takes you through the planning process and gives you a model that you can adapt to other questions.

> How much did attitudes to conscientious objectors change from the First World War to the Second World War?
>
> **[16 marks]**

Step 1: Planning your answer

First make it clear what changes happened and when. Use a quick plan to organise your thinking. This will give you a clear, simple structure to your answer. Do not worry about more than two or three examples for each period – you will not have time to write about any more.

This question is asking you to compare, analyse and evaluate attitudes to conscientious objectors in two periods. It is a challenging question, so use the advice that follows to produce an effective answer.

The danger is that you simply end up describing each period. One of the problems students have is that they get so involved in showing the examiner all the interesting facts they have revised about a topic that they lose track and forget to focus on the question!

STOP Do not lose sight of the question or the big picture

The examiner does not want you to tell them everything you know about the topic or time period.

They **do** want you to show that you can use what you know to analyse and evaluate just how much attitudes changed in each period. The key is to focus on the type of question: **How much did attitudes to_____change?** Were the attitudes to COs the same by the Second World War or had some attitudes changed? The steps that follow will help you to see the overall picture and make a clear decision.

The exam will include some bullet points, which are there to help you think. However, there is a danger they will limit your own ideas. If you don't recognise what is included there is also a danger you will lose confidence in your own skills! One positive strategy is to cover them up and do your own plan. Once this is done (or if you are stuck) you should look at the bullet points to see if you have missed anything out. It is your own knowledge that you should focus on – not the bullet points!

STOP Danger: bullet points!

Think about the First World War first. Was there just one attitude or were there different opinions between law makers and the authorities and ordinary people? Then do the same for the Second World War. Use a double bubble diagram (below) to help you plan and identify changes/continuity.

Then work out how you are going to structure your answer – will you go for a chronological approach or will you be bold and write one paragraph on changed attitudes and the second paragraph on continuities?

Step 2: Evaluating each change

As you write your answer, **describe** each changed attitude, back it up with evidence and **explain** the significance of the changing attitude. It is the explanation that will gain you lots of marks. Some technical words you might like to use when you write your answer are:

Revolution – a complete or dramatic change
Catalyst – it speeds up change
Development – something that builds on what was done already
Rapid change – a large number of changes in a short time
Gradual change – a slow pace to changes
Turning point – it totally changes the way things are done in the future

> Attitudes to conscientious objectors changed to an extent.

> One big change was the attitudes of the law makers. For example in the First World War they had military officers running the tribunals which decided about COs. One of these said 'you are only fit to be on the end of a German bayonet' which shows you their negative attitude. In the Second World War the tribunals were run by civilians, who did not have such an attitude towards them. Even the Prime Minister himself said there should be 'no persecution' of COs. This shows us there was quite a dramatic change in attitude, perhaps it was because COs had been seen doing useful work in the First World War.
> However attitudes of the press and some of the public had not changed very much. For example ...

Step 3: Make the final decision

Now you need to decide just how much attitudes had changed. You need to make a clear judgement or you will not have fully answered the question. Which decision makes the most sense to you? A basic adjective like 'great' or 'small' would be enough here – it is still a valid judgement!

You also need to explain your decision. If you have mentioned a turning point it would be worth discussing in your conclusion.

Activities

Unlike in the exam, you have plenty of time to plan for this style of question. In pairs, go through steps 1–3 about attitudes to conscientious objectors in the First and Second World Wars.

1   **Plan the changes** in attitudes to conscientious objectors in the First and Second World Wars. It will be helpful if you identify changes and continuity in your plan. As you have time, you should also include the evidence that you will use in your answer on your plan. Don't waste precious time doing this in the exam though!
2   Write your answer and **evaluate the changes**.
3   **Make the final decision** in your short conclusion.

Clearly organised – this student has planned, yet hasn't wasted time on a lengthy introduction. By saying 'to an extent', they are showing they will discuss what changed but also what stayed the same.

Plenty of good explanation here. The planning has certainly helped the student to stay focused on the question. There is good use of evidence from both wars. The use of the contrasting connective 'however' shows this will be a balanced answer.

Practice questions

Try using this Exam Buster strategy to help you answer these exam questions:

1   How different was the way the crime of witchcraft was treated in the 16th century compared to the 18th century?
2   How much did the system of law and order change from the Anglo-Saxon period to the Norman period?

Activities

You could also try using these skills to help you think in more detail about the extent of change in some of the topics from the core part of your course:

1   When did prisons change more: the 19th century or the 20th century?
2   When did policing change more: the 19th century or the 20th century?

> Overall attitudes changed a _____ amount.

> The greatest amount of change was in ...

Did changing attitudes to women mean changes in the law?

These pages show a large amount of information. Your task is to use this to put together a living graph to look at the laws made about women in the last 100 years – do these laws match the changing attitudes to women in Britain?

In 1900 women received different treatment from men in the legal system. It was best summed up by the 18th-century legal writer William Blackstone who said 'the very being or legal existence of the woman is suspended during the marriage', meaning a woman was not a person in her own right but simply part of her husband.

Today men and women are equal – clearly a great deal has changed in the last 100 years. In particular, during the past 40 years, laws to do with domestic violence have been passed to protect women from abuse. (Laws have also recently been passed to protect men suffering from domestic violence.) Knowing these laws is an important part of this extension unit. However, it is also important to know how they fit into the bigger picture of women's rights and their changing position within the legal system. There is a lot to discover here!

Your enquiry needs to focus on:

- how the laws changed to protect women, particularly after the 1970s
- how much these laws fit into the overall pattern of changing attitudes towards women in the century
- deciding which factors were important in making these changes.

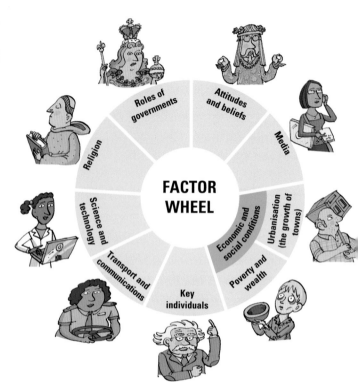

FACTOR WHEEL

Roles of governments · Attitudes and beliefs · Media · Urbanisation (the growth of towns) · Economic and social conditions · Poverty and wealth · Key individuals · Transport and communications · Science and technology · Religion

Activities

1 In this activity you will be creating a living graph. Work in pairs and look at the wide range of information on pages 113–115. Your first task is to organise it chronologically (in date order).

2 Draw a graph like the one below in the centre of an A3 sheet of paper, with space to write above and below the horizontal timeline. You will need to work out if each piece of information shows a positive or negative change for women and write it above or below the timeline in chronological order.

⊕
⊖ | LIVING GRAPH

3 Circle the **laws about women** in one colour to link them together.

4 Circle any laws or events just to do with **domestic violence** in a second colour. This is often called a hidden crime as there is no specific charge for domestic violence, lots of other laws are used.

5 Look at your graph. When did the laws start to change and make it clear that abuse was not going to be tolerated?

6 New laws often reflect new attitudes. Now circle any examples of **attitudes to women** in a third colour to link them together. Look at your graph. What does this tell us – are there positive changes or some worrying continuity?

7 Your living graph is now complete. Overall, how do the laws around domestic violence match the changing attitudes to women in the legal system in the 20th century?

8 Now look at the factor wheel. Which factors most help us understand why these changes happened when they did?

1971 Jack Ashley was the first MP to discuss domestic violence in Parliament. At first the authorities, including the police, were reluctant to take this issue more seriously. They thought it would take time away from 'serious' crimes.

2004 Statistics show that one-quarter of women and one-sixth of men suffer from domestic violence during their lives. Each week two women are killed by their current or ex-partners.

1962 First female County Court judge.

1975 Maternity pay introduced: women could no longer be sacked for being pregnant.

1983 The charity Refuge set up a 24-hour helpline for victims of domestic violence.

2009 The Crown Prosecution Service released fresh guidelines showing exactly how different sorts of domestic violence match crimes that can be taken to court – including harassment, assault and murder.

1967 Abortion Act: before this it is estimated that up to 15 per cent of all pregnancy-related deaths were due to illegal abortions.

1991 Rape within marriage was classified as a crime for the first time in England and Wales.

1988 First female Law Lord – at the top of the legal system.

1975 Sex discrimination now illegal in the workplace.

1921 The Football Association banned women from playing in league grounds.

1918 Women over 30 granted the right to vote – all men over 21 could vote.

1928 Women over 21 granted the right to vote.

1987 The police set up their first domestic violence unit.

◄ Even in the 1950s many people still thought women should be housewives. The caption to this cartoon read: 'I'm afraid you will have to fend for yourselves quite a lot now children – your mother has been elected to the council.'

1996 Family Law Act meant that arrest was automatic if violence had even been threatened in a domestic situation.

MURDER in Manchester

A woman was murdered by her husband in Manchester in 2008. She had called the police 11 times about him, but they did not link the calls. He is now serving life in prison. The police admitted that even though they have improved their approach to domestic violence, they still have much to do.

1921 Unemployment benefit was given to wives for the first time.

1971 First women's safe house set up by the charity Refuge.

1923 A woman could divorce her husband if he had committed adultery – a man was already able to do this. In 1937 this was extended to include drunkenness and cruelty. This was the first legal way out of an abusive relationship.

1976 Domestic Violence Act. Courts could protect victims of domestic violence for the first time. Domestic violence was now officially a crime. Victims could get restraining orders to stop harassment. They could also get court orders to exclude abusers from the family home.

2010 Every police force has a domestic violence 'champion' and there are now special courts set up to deal with this crime.

1919 Nancy Astor was the first female MP to sit in the House of Parliament. She later said 'women have got to make the world safe for men since men have made it so darned unsafe for women'.

1998 The Zero Tolerance Trust surveyed 2,000 young people in England and Wales. Fifty per cent of boys and 33 per cent of girls said it was sometimes acceptable for a man to hit a woman – for example if she nagged too much. What does this tell you about the extent of changing attitudes?

Source 2

ANDY CAPP

"I was talkin' when I should 'ave been listenin' "

▲ This cartoon character could be seen in the *Daily Mirror* newspaper. This particular cartoon was published on 13 February 1958.

2005 Only 4 per cent of reported incidents of domestic violence result in a conviction.

1922 Connie Morrison became the first female solicitor.

1979 Margaret Thatcher was Britain's first female Prime Minister.

In the 1950s and 60s the 'joke' was often about domestic violence. Today it would not be acceptable for a newspaper to make a joke about this serious crime. What does this tell you about the attitudes some people had to domestic violence in the past? How much have attitudes changed today?

1922 Helena Normanton was the first-ever female barrister.

1933 The BBC stopped employing married women.

1929 Women legally became 'persons' in law.

1942 Women no longer had to wear hats in church.

1920 Oxford University admitted women for the first time.

Source 3

The attitudes of some judges were a problem. In 1988 one judge did **not** jail a man who sexually assaulted his step-daughter. The judge said the crime was less serious because he was a 'healthy young husband' whose wife had gone off sex (due to a pregnancy). Some other judges in the 1970s and 80s showed similar attitudes.

1919 Sex Disqualification Removal Act meant women could now be lawyers, civil servants and vets.

1970 Equal Pay Act – women could not be paid less than the lowest paid man. Many companies still paid women less for the same job.

1896 '[If women got the vote] political power in many large cities would chiefly be in the hands of young, ill-educated, giddy, and often ill-conducted girls.' Frederick Rylands.

1922 Infanticide Act. A woman suffering from post-natal depression could not be executed for murdering her child.

2009 Statistics show that men still earn on average 22 per cent more than women – this is called the Gender Pay Gap.

1944 Women could keep working as teachers after they were married.

1974 National Women's Aid Federation set up to co-ordinate support services for women.

2003 Over 60,000 calls a year were made to the Refuge helpline.

1911 International Women's Day was held for the first time. Now groups such as Amnesty International campaign on this day to raise awareness of violence against women across the world.

2004 Domestic Violence Act passed – this increased powers for courts. Restraining orders can be put on anyone charged with violence, even if they are acquitted. If the restraining orders are broken offenders can be sent to prison for up to five years. Those charged can also be sent on behaviour rehabilitation courses. This law gave male and female victims the same level of protection as a study found that one-sixth of men have also suffered from domestic violence.

The examiners are not trying to catch you out: they are trying to give you a chance to show what you know – **and what you can do with what you know**. If you can work out what the question is getting at, you will probably be able to answer it from what you have learned.

To make sure your answer stays relevant to the question on the exam paper you will need to practise how to decode questions.

Decoding exam questions

Step 1: Read the question a couple of times.

Step 2: Highlight each of the following. You could use a different colour for each.

> **Date boundaries** – what time period should you cover in your answer? Stick to this carefully otherwise you will waste time writing about events that are not relevant to the question.
>
> **Content focus** – the topic the examiner wants you to focus on.
>
> **Question type** – different question types require different approaches. Look for key words, like 'describe' or 'explain', that will help you work out what type of approach is needed.
>
> **Marks available** – look at how many marks the question is worth. This gives you a guide as to how much you are expected to write. Do not spend too long on questions that are only worth a few marks.

Look at the exam question below.

You need to 'describe the key features' of the laws. You are not being asked to 'explain why' they were introduced or whether you think they were effective.

The content focus for this question is the laws to do with domestic violence. This must be the focus of your answer. There is no need to explore other areas of women's rights such as voting or the workplace.

Describe the key features of the laws regarding domestic violence in the late 20th century. [9 marks]

You must stick to the date boundaries of the question. In this case it is late 20th century – from the 1970s onwards. Details of laws before this will not gain you any extra marks.

9 marks are available. This indicates that a more developed answer is required. You need more than bullet points or a short paragraph but not a long essay.

Tackling 'key features' questions

Tip 1: Give specific details and link what you say to the question

An effective answer to a 'key features' question like: **'Describe the key features of the laws to do with domestic violence after 1970'** means more than writing a list of the measures introduced. The answer below would **not** get many marks.

The first two sentences are general statements. They provide no specific detail.

> In the 20th century people believed it was important to stop domestic violence. They introduced many laws. They used punishments like restriction orders and prison and court orders.

The last sentence is a list of punishments. The student does not explain how they link to any specific law. A general list of punishments is not good enough if you want to achieve higher level marks.

This student would gain more marks if she linked punishments to actual laws, and showed how the laws developed over the decades. Look at the example below. It mentions fewer punishments but it gains more marks. This is because the student gives **precise details** about laws and punishments and **links the key features** of different laws, focusing on the use of restraining orders.

> The first law to deal with domestic violence was in 1976. This gave judges the power to prosecute men for this crime for the first time. They could use restraining orders to keep abusers away from the family home. Then in 2004 this was increased. Even if someone was found not guilty of the crime, the judge could still put a restraining order on them if they felt the victims were at risk. Lastly, the guidelines about linking domestic violence to assault were made clear in 2009, so that judges could use sronger punishments.

Tip 2: Stay relevant to the question

One of the main problems with 'key features' questions is that students write too much! They include details that are not relevant to the question.

Activity

Read the answer below. The student has written too much because he has not stayed relevant to the question. He clearly knows about the topic but is not focused enough! On your own copy, cross out the sentences that are irrelevant to the question. If you take out the parts that do not answer the question you should be left with a good answer!

> Domestic violence is something that up to one-quarter of all women experience. But it has only been a crime since the Domestic Violence Act of 1976, and was only mentioned in Parliament for the first time ever in 1971. Before that the only escape women had was by getting a divorce for cruelty. In fact women had only had the vote since 1918, and the first woman MP was only in 1919 so it is not surprising that laws to protect them took a long time to happen.
>
> The Domestic Violence Act of 1976 gave the courts the power to use restraining orders on abusive men. They could also prevent men from having access to the family home. However the attitude of some of the judges was not helpful and seemed to be against the women. On one occasion a man was not even sent to jail for abusing his step-daughter. Attitudes still needed to change.
>
> Charities like Refuge were set up to look after women and families who were suffering from abuse. They even set up a 24-hour hotline. This hotline gets over 60,000 calls each year. Nowadays, other charities like Amnesty International campaign for women around the world on this issue. They use International Women's Day to get their message across.

Tip 3: Practice makes perfect!

As you continue with your GCSE course make sure that you continue to practise 'key features' questions. You can use the examples below.

- Describe the key features of the trials and punishments of witches.
- Describe the key features of the laws to do with Conscientious Objectors.

Section 7: Conclusion: How have the factors affected change in crime and punishment?

While you have been studying crime and punishment you will have noticed that a number of 'factors' that affect change have cropped up again and again. Our task in History is not just to list or describe events from the past, but also to explain why they happened. These factors help us with those explanations.

You might have noticed that one factor stands out as a very significant one, bringing change in almost every period: the role of government.

Government

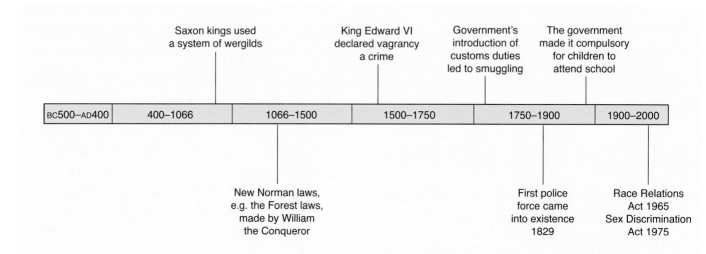

| | Saxon kings used a system of wergilds | | King Edward VI declared vagrancy a crime | Government's introduction of customs duties led to smuggling | The government made it compulsory for children to attend school |

| BC500–AD400 | 400–1066 | 1066–1500 | 1500–1750 | 1750–1900 | 1900–2000 |

New Norman laws, e.g. the Forest laws, made by William the Conqueror

First police force came into existence 1829

Race Relations Act 1965 Sex Discrimination Act 1975

Governments have a massive influence on crime and punishment. They:

- decide what is a crime
- set the punishments
- enforce the law.

Some historians say that the best deterrent to crime is not harsh punishment, but the likelihood of getting caught. One factor in the fall in crime from the mid-19th century could be the growth of effective police forces in Britain.

Roles of government

Activity

Complete and fill out a table like this one with examples from each period of government. You can use the sources from this book.

Period	Deciding what is a crime	Setting the punishments	Enforcing the law
Saxon			
Late Middle Ages			
Early Modern Period			
Industrial Britain			
20th century			

What other factors have affected crime?

Poverty and wealth

Crime often increases when poverty increases. But the link is not simple. Not everyone who is poor turns to crime – for example during the 1930s Depression. Other factors, such as the personality of the individual, or the likelihood of getting caught, play their part. It may not be poverty itself, but greater inequality between rich and poor, which causes crime.

The cost of punishment has always been important. Throughout history, prisons were regarded as too expensive until, in 19th-century Britain, greater national wealth meant that the country could afford to build prisons. Transportation was ended partly because it was becoming too expensive. Governments today are looking for cheaper alternatives to prison.

Urbanisation (the growth of towns)

Crime rates have always been higher in urban areas, including, for example, in ancient Rome. In Section 5 you saw how 19th-century cities grew very fast. They provided plenty of opportunities for crime, for getting away unrecognised and for getting rid of the stolen goods. The system of policing was based on life in villages and was hopelessly inadequate for cities.

Attitudes and beliefs

Beliefs and attitudes have had a major impact too. Look at the timeline below. Do any of these cross over with the impact of government?

Activities

1. Make two large copies of the factor wheel; each should fill a page of A4 paper.
2. Label one factor wheel 'Factors affecting crime'. Look at the information about governments on page 118 and write down anything that explains how this factor has influenced crime in your 'roles of government' section on your factor wheel. Then do the same with the sections on 'poverty and wealth', 'urbanisation' and 'attitudes and beliefs'.
3. Label the other factor wheel 'Factors affecting punishment' and repeat question 2, but looking at how these factors have influenced punishment.
4. Now look at the empty factors on your wheels. For each one, find an example from this book of how it influenced crime and punishment and write it in that factor section to complete your factor wheels.
5. Find some examples of crime and punishment being influenced by more than one factor. Add link-lines to show how factors work together.

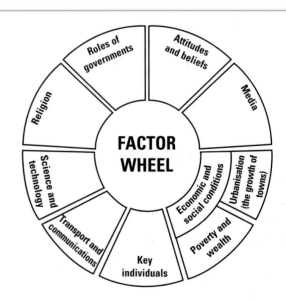

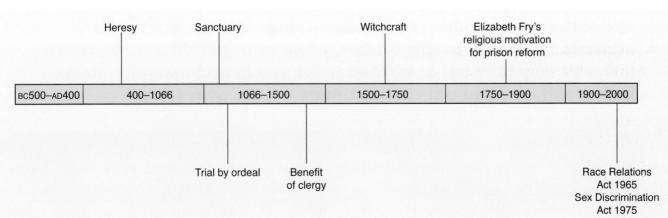

Source Enquiry:
Protest, law and order in the 20th century

You are now entering a different kind of unit.

This may look like it is part of your Development Study –
BUT IT IS NOT!

What you have learned in the Development Study will be useful
background knowledge, but Edexcel Unit 3 is more about developing
your enquiry skills and your ability to use sources as evidence.

Protest, law and order is the case study that provides examples for
you to use when developing these skills.

REMEMBER: SOURCES first, **PROTEST** second.

Why study Protest?
The right to protest is part of living in a democracy. Protest is
one of the ways people try to change things that are wrong. So
understanding why people protest, whether or not their protests are
just, and why they fail or succeed helps you to understand protests
better, and how you can change things in your own society.

20th-century protests: the big picture

Suffragettes 1903 to 1914

Before 1918 women were not allowed to vote for members of Parliament. By 1900 women had begun to protest about this. They did this in different ways, but most were peaceful. The Suffragettes were founded in 1903. They used more violent methods of protest such as smashing windows, and were harshly dealt with by the authorities.

Your enquiry: Why did Suffragette protest turn violent?

General Strike 1926

In 1926 coal miners went on strike over their pay and working conditions. Later that year many other workers joined a General Strike (a strike involving a range of industries) to support the coal miners. Rail workers stopped delivering coal and dockers stopped unloading ships. The strike lasted only just over a week but was one of the most dramatic political events of the 1920s. The government accused the strikers of being revolutionaries and used soldiers or volunteers to do some of the essential jobs that the strikers would not do.

Your enquiry: Why did the General Strike collapse so quickly?

Poll Tax 1990

The Poll Tax was a new tax paid by every person in Britain, whatever they earned. This led to mass protests, including rioting in central London in 1990. The protests succeeded and the Poll Tax was abolished. Soon after, Prime Minister Margaret Thatcher resigned. The campaign was well organised and had very broad support throughout Britain.

Your enquiry: Why was the Poll Tax protest successful in achieving its aims?

Miners' Strike 1984

Margaret Thatcher's government decided to close loss-making coal mines. When plans were announced the coal miners went on strike. The strikers did not get the support of other unions: they did not even get the support of all the miners, but the strike lasted a year. There were pitched battles with police. In the end poverty drove the miners back to work.

Your enquiry: What made the Miners' Strike such a bitter dispute?

Activities

Which protest?
1 Read the four descriptions on this page. Which of the four protests do you think is shown in the photograph?
2 How do you know?
3 What else does the photograph tell you about this protest?
4 What else would you like to find out about each of these four protests?

A chart like this will help you remember the key features of each protest. You could make an enormous chart that compared all four protests or you could make a new chart for each protest.

smarter revision: protest checklist

Who was protesting?

Why were they protesting?

Who led the protest?

When was the protest?

What tactics did the protesters use?

How was the protest **organised**?

What part did **the media** play in the protest?

How did **the authorities** react to the protest?

What were **the results** of the protest?

What sources have been most useful in understanding this protest?

meet the examiner

Examine that question – analyses each kind of question you will face.

How to – takes you step by step through the process of using and evaluating sources and answering exam questions on sources.

Improve that answer – gives you sample answers and asks you to mark them or improve them.

Warning – helps you avoid the most common mistakes.

Smarter Revision: Factor chart

Throughout the development study (Unit 1) you were looking for how different factors affected the development of Crime and Punishment. In this Source Enquiry you are still interested in factors – in particular those in the wheel opposite. Some of the sources and questions in your examination paper might be about the influence of these factors, so use a chart like this to record examples of how a factor influenced the outcome of the protest. We have done some examples for you.

Factors	Leadership	Organisation	Communication and media	Government/the authorities
Questions to consider	- How did leaders influence the protest? - What made the leaders successful or unsuccessful?	- How well organised were the protesters/the authorities? - How did organisation affect the outcome?	- How well did the protesters/authorities communicate? - How did mass media influence public perception of the protest?	- What resources were available to the government? - How did decisions made by government or authorities affect the outcome?
The Suffragettes	- The Pankhursts were strong leaders. They inspired both loyalty and hatred. - They were involved and led by example rather than being 'behind the scenes'. For instance they got themselves arrested and joined in hunger strikes.			- The government decision to send Suffragettes to prison and later to force feed them increased sympathy for the Suffragettes.
The General Strike		- The General Strike started before the Trade Unions had really got themselves organised for it. - The government on the other hand had spent months preparing for it and organising for a General Strike.		- The Government had massive resources available to them. They could use the army and the police to break the strike and had trained extra 'special constables' beforehand.
The Miners' Strike		- The Miners' Strike was much better organised than the General Strike. Plans were in place to organise mass pickets and support the miners through a long strike.	- The TV cameras were there for all the major events and showed the violence at picket lines. - At the 'Battle of Orgreave' both sides thought the mass media were biased against them!	
The Poll Tax Protest	- Margaret Thatcher made it her personal crusade to introduce the Poll Tax. She did not listen to the advice of others who said it would be impossible to implement.		- There was a strong local network of Anti-Poll Tax Unions that had been set up in the main cities, based on existing community and political groups such as Militant.	

The Source Enquiry is an important exam, worth 25 per cent of your final mark – the same percentage as the Development Study. The Source Enquiry exam has six to eight sources and five questions testing your skills in using sources as evidence. This exam paper and the sources booklet on pages 126–127 show you the kind of questions and sources the exam might contain.

Unit 3: Schools History Project Source Enquiry

Option 3B: Protest, law and order in the twentieth century

① Time: 1 hour 15 minutes
The total mark for this paper is 50.

Background information

② In 1925 the owners of Britain's coal mines announced plans to cut miners' pay and increase their working hours. The miners' trade union decided to strike in protest against the changes. In 1926 the Trades Union Congress agreed to support the miners and called a General Strike. This means they asked workers from all industries across the country to go on strike in support of the miners. This General Strike lasted for nine days although the miners' strike carried on for another nine months. The aims of the strike were not achieved. When the miners returned to work they had to accept longer hours and lower wages.

The authorities (the mine owners and the government) had prepared well beforehand because they were expecting the strike, and used various methods to defeat it. The sources for this paper give you a range of views on the strike and allow you to make up your own mind why it failed.

---

① TIMING

The marks for **each** question are shown in brackets. Use this as a guide to how much time to spend on each question.

It is important to time yourself carefully. Some students run out of time because they spend too long on the first two questions and don't have time for the higher mark questions that come later. So stick to a time plan like this:

- Approx 5 minutes: Read all the questions, the background information and scan the sources so that you pick up the theme of the paper and how the questions and the sources relate to each other.
- No more than 20 minutes: Questions 1 and 2 (14 marks)
- Approx 25 minutes: Questions 3 and 4 (20 marks)
- Approx 20 minutes: Question 5 (16 marks)
- Approx 5 minutes: Check your answers. If time is really short check your answer to Question 5 first. This is where the examiner will be looking particularly closely at your spelling, punctuation and grammar.

② THE BACKGROUND INFORMATION

This is an important part of the exam paper and shouldn't be overlooked. Study it carefully even if you know the topic really well because you can use it to put the sources for the paper into context. Highlight important points and identify the theme of the paper. Here the theme is an investigation into why the strike failed, and it draws your attention to how organised the government were. Does this explain the failure or were there other factors?

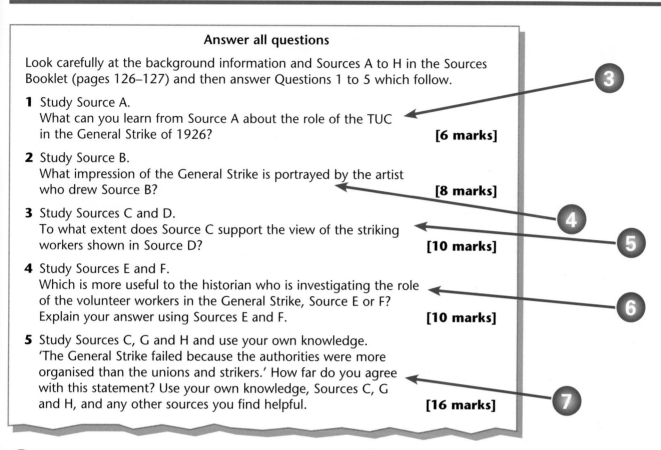

Answer all questions

Look carefully at the background information and Sources A to H in the Sources Booklet (pages 126–127) and then answer Questions 1 to 5 which follow.

1 Study Source A.
What can you learn from Source A about the role of the TUC in the General Strike of 1926? **[6 marks]**

2 Study Source B.
What impression of the General Strike is portrayed by the artist who drew Source B? **[8 marks]**

3 Study Sources C and D.
To what extent does Source C support the view of the striking workers shown in Source D? **[10 marks]**

4 Study Sources E and F.
Which is more useful to the historian who is investigating the role of the volunteer workers in the General Strike, Source E or F? Explain your answer using Sources E and F. **[10 marks]**

5 Study Sources C, G and H and use your own knowledge.
'The General Strike failed because the authorities were more organised than the unions and strikers.' How far do you agree with this statement? Use your own knowledge, Sources C, G and H, and any other sources you find helpful. **[16 marks]**

3 DEVELOPING INFERENCES FROM A SOURCE

The first question will usually be an inference question. You need to go beyond the obvious clues in the source and explain what you can learn from the source. The Exam Buster on pages 134–135 helps you tackle 'inference questions' effectively.

4 ANALYSING THE WAY AN EVENT OR PERSON IS PORTRAYED IN A SOURCE

The emphasis in these questions is on how an impression has been deliberately created by the person who produced the source. Advice on how to tackle 'portrayal questions' can be found on pages 142–143.

5 CROSS-REFERENCING SOURCES

This question is asking you to compare what is being said in two sources and to reach a judgement on how far they are saying the same thing. The Exam Buster on pages 150–151 helps you tackle 'cross-referencing' questions.

6 EVALUATING THE USEFULNESS OF SOURCES

This type of question asks you to evaluate how useful two sources are for a particular historical enquiry; in this case, the role of the volunteer workers. You need to explore the strengths and weaknesses of each source before reaching an overall judgement on which source is the more useful. The Exam Buster on pages 158–159 helps you tackle this type of question.

7 USING SOURCES TO REACH A JUDGEMENT

The final question asks you to use the sources and your own knowledge to evaluate an interpretation or point of view. In this case you must decide the extent to which you agree or disagree with this statement and use the source to support your judgement. The Exam Buster on pages 160–161 helps you to tackle this type of question effectively.

The question directs you to use Sources C, G and H, so you must use those. However you can also use any other source on the paper to support your answer. The specified sources will always contain evidence for and against the statement.

Before you answer this question, a good tip is to go through the sources and place a tick or cross in the margin when you find evidence that either supports or contradicts the statement.

SOURCES BOOKLET

Source A

An extract from a press statement from the Trades Union Congress Press and Publicity Committee. The statement was issued on 1 May 1926, following a special conference of trade union executives to approve plans for a 'national' strike in defence of the miners. It describes preparations for the General Strike due to begin on 3 May 1926.

> The General Council of the Trade Union Congress (TUC) met after the Conference on Saturday and completed its arrangements for dealing with the present situation. Certain committees were appointed and preparations made to meet possible contingencies [unplanned events]. The General Council of the TUC is making arrangements for direct communication with other trade unions and announcements will be made directly to them. The General Council warns the workers and their unions to take no notice of any statement that may be broadcast by wireless [radio] or circulated in any other form.

Source B

UNDER WHICH FLAG?

John Bull. "ONE OF THESE TWO FLAGS HAS GOT TO COME DOWN—AND IT WON'T BE MINE."

▲ A cartoon that appeared in *Punch* magazine on 12 May 1926.

Source C

From the *Guardian* newspaper published Thursday 6 May 1926, describing events in Leeds when protesters and police clashed.

> Ugly scenes were witnessed in the chief thoroughfares of Leeds about noon today. The trouble began when several thousand strikers attacked one of the emergency tram-cars with lumps of coal taken from a passing lorry, a number of windows in the tram-car being smashed and passengers having narrow escapes. The strikers rushed towards another tram-car a moment later, but were held back for a time by a strong body of police.
>
> Amid loud cries of 'down with the police', the strikers rushed on to them. The police backed to a narrower thoroughfare, where they defended themselves with their batons. About 5,000 strong, the strikers dashed round another street, but the police, who had been reinforced, managed to keep them clear by their truncheons.

Source D

▲ Pickets in Crewe try to stop a railway clerk going to work, 10 May 1926.

Source E

Daily Mail

WEDNESDAY 5 MAY 1926

| **FIRST DAY OF THE STRIKE** | REFUSALS TO GO OUT ON STRIKE | Vehicles Wrecked by London Mob | **HOW LONDONERS WENT TO WORK** | Plenty of Food and Transport |

▲ Headlines from the front page of the *Daily Mail* newspaper, 5 May 1926.

Source F

A 'volunteer worker' describes his experiences during the General Strike. Many professional and middle-class people became 'volunteers' to transport food and other essential supplies. This interview was recorded in the 1980s for a local newspaper.

> We were put up in army barracks and called at about 3a.m. the next morning, probably to avoid trouble with the pickets. We were told to drive lorries, large army trucks, each with a policeman and a soldier on board. We learned later that each soldier had only one bullet in his rifle. Our destination was the London docks where we were to offload food from ships in order to relieve the nationwide shortage. The eighteen trucks in our group drove by roundabout routes, to avoid confrontation with the strikers, to where the army was waiting for us and apparently setting up some type of system to handle food.

Source G

Philip Snowden was a Labour MP during the General Strike. The following extract is from his autobiography written in 1934.

> During the nine days of the strike I remained silent. From one point of view I was not sorry that this experiment had been tried. The Trade Unions needed a lesson of the futility and foolishness of such a trial of strength. A general strike could in no circumstances be successful. A general strike is an attempt to hold up the community, and against such an attempt the community will mobilise all its resources. There is no country in the world which has proportionally such a large middle-class population as Great Britain. They, with the help of governmental organisation, with a million motor-cars at their service, could defeat any strike on a large scale which threatened the vital services.

Source H

◀ A photograph of milk lorries driving through London under armed guard during the General Strike.

127

Arson, window-smashing, hunger strikes! These methods of protest would cause a stir at any time. But imagine the outcry from public, media and government when a group of otherwise law-abiding, middle-class women used these methods in order to win the right to vote. Your enquiry is to consider why Suffragette protest turned so violent. Did they plan this to happen or were they responding to the way the authorities dealt with their protests?

Women in 1900

At the end of the 19th century, women in Britain still had few rights. The Victorian ideal for a middle class woman was to care for her home and family and follow the wishes of her husband or father, who was also, in most cases, financially responsible for her.

However, by 1900 more women were being educated and many went to work and paid taxes. Some laws had been passed to improve their individual rights. Women could vote in local elections but they still were not allowed to vote in national elections (called 'suffrage'). Many men, and many women too, believed women should not vote in such important elections because women were incapable of making informed decisions.

Suffragists – meeting, marching, lobbying

Campaigners for women's suffrage believed that winning the right to vote was important because then (male) political leaders would have to take notice of women and pass laws to improve women's rights in other areas of life. In 1897, several campaigning groups united together as the National Union of Women's Suffrage Societies (NUWSS) under the leadership of Millicent Fawcett. They were known as 'Suffragists'. They believed in peaceful campaigning. They used tactics such as marches, petitions, leaflets and letters to newspapers to get the public on their side. They lobbied MPs (writing letters to and meeting them) to persuade them to support their cause. They wanted to show how respectable and serious they were. They thought that if they presented their case in a clear way success would follow. These tactics were successful to a degree. The Suffragists got more and more MPs on their side but never enough to pass a law giving women the vote.

Source 1

From *The Times*, 4 October 1905.

Last night the Liberals held a meeting in Manchester. Sir Edward Grey, the Foreign Secretary, was to speak. Miss Christabel Pankhurst got up from her chair and shouted, 'Will you give votes to women?' Sir Edward replied, 'This is a party matter which I am not prepared to discuss.' Miss Pankhurst was then forcibly ejected from the meeting.

Suffragettes – seeking publicity

Many Suffragists were frustrated by the NUWSS campaign and felt they needed to use more militant tactics. 'Militant' means aggressive and confrontational. In 1903 Emmeline Pankhurst started a new organisation in Manchester called the Women's Social and Political Union (WSPU). Men could not join – only women. Their motto was 'Deeds not Words'. Their aim was to attract maximum publicity and mount a campaign that no one could ignore (see Source 1). The *Daily Mail* nicknamed them 'Suffragettes'.

In 1906 the Suffragettes moved offices to London to be nearer Parliament, the courts of law and the newspapers. Whenever Parliament was about to debate the issue of women's suffrage they organised meetings, marches and demonstrations. They also published their own newspaper, *Votes for Women*, and made posters.

Parliament was the main focus of their direct action. In March 1906 they tried to meet Prime Minister Henry Campbell-Bannerman at 10 Downing Street. When they were asked to leave, one woman leapt onto the roof of a car and made a speech outside the building. In October 1906 leading Suffragettes entered the lobby area at Parliament and made speeches to the MPs, which was illegal. As police officers removed one speaker, another took her place, calling on MPs to give women the vote. In the end ten women were charged and ordered to either 'keep the peace' for six months or go to prison for two months. They chose prison. Such public confrontation was a very different approach from the Suffragists, but the arrests and the prison sentences earned the WSPU a lot of sympathy, plus new funds and new members.

The Suffragettes may have been very dissatisfied that they had not yet got the vote but they had succeeded in making the headlines.

Emmeline Pankhurst

- Born in 1858 in Manchester to a well-off family
- Married to a lawyer (died 1889); together they had five children
- Formed WSPU in 1903 with daughters Christabel and Sylvia as co-leaders
- Renowned as a great speaker
- Arrested many times for violent protests
- While in prison went on hunger strike many times
- Died in 1928 shortly after women granted equal voting rights to men
- Daughter Sylvia was more radical than Emmeline and encouraged the development of militancy.

Source 2

2 What is the attitude of the cartoonist to the Suffragists and Suffragettes?

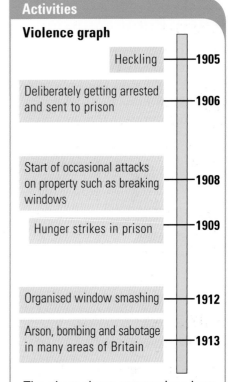

1 Which figure represents a Suffragist/Suffragette?

3 Do you think Emmeline Pankhurst would have been pleased to see this cartoon?

THE SHRIEKING SISTER.

THE SENSIBLE WOMAN. "YOU HELP OUR CAUSE? WHY, YOU'RE ITS WORST ENEMY!"

▲ A cartoon from *Punch* magazine in 1906. *Punch* was a popular weekly magazine for middle- and upper-class people.

Activities

Violence graph

Heckling	1905
Deliberately getting arrested and sent to prison	1906
Start of occasional attacks on property such as breaking windows	1908
Hunger strikes in prison	1909
Organised window smashing	1912
Arson, bombing and sabotage in many areas of Britain	1913

The chart above summarises how violence increased. Over the next six pages you will make your own graph to help explain the increasing violence of the Suffragette campaign. Add annotations in one colour to show actions by the Suffragettes that increased the violence, and in another colour to show actions by others which increased the violence.

1 Use all the information from pages 128–129 to complete the graph up to 1906.

2 Discuss: in what ways are these Suffragette tactics different from the tactics of the Suffragists?

How and why did the protest become more violent after 1906?

One lesson the Suffragettes learned from the events of 1906 was that being sent to prison earned them sympathy and support. So they recruited women from their membership who were willing to deliberately get sent to prison. In 1907 a Suffragette march on Parliament was blocked by police on horses. As women tried to push on through they were arrested. This was the most violent event so far and over 50 women were sent to prison.

A new Prime Minister

In April 1908, the Liberals elected a new leader, Herbert Asquith, as Prime Minister. Although many Liberals supported women's suffrage, Asquith did not. He told the Suffragists and Suffragettes that it was up to them to prove that there was support for votes for women. In response, in June 1908, they staged the biggest procession ever seen. Half a million women marched to Hyde Park in London on 'Women's Sunday' on 21 June. They felt they had proved their case but Asquith did nothing.

Window smashing

On 30 June 1908, a peaceful demonstration in Parliament Square in London turned nasty when heavy-handed tactics were used by 5,000 policemen. Enraged by the police action, two teachers threw stones through the windows of 10 Downing Street. They were sent to Holloway Prison for two months; on release they were greeted as heroines. Twenty-seven other women had also been sent to prison. Frustration and anger mounted. Women pestered politicians and disrupted political meetings, so were banned from them. A demonstration and planned 'rush' to force entry into the House of Commons led to violent clashes and arrests.

By the autumn of 1909 the NUWSS (the suffragists) felt that the violence and militant tactics of the Suffragettes – abusing politicians, rowdy demonstrations, throwing missiles at the police – were damaging the cause and putting off sympathisers. They distanced themselves from the Suffragettes.

Source 3

From the *New York Times*, published 2 July 1908.

The extraordinary demonstration last night before the Houses of Parliament made by the Suffragettes had a rather startling sequel today, when one of the women, Mary Leigh, arrested for breaking windows in the house of Prime Minister Asquith, declared in the Bow Street Court that 'the next time we come out you can expect bombs'. Mrs Mary Leigh was sentenced to two months' hard labour.

Source 4

Comments made in court by Emmeline Pankhurst in 1908.

We have tried every way. We have presented larger petitions than were ever presented before for any other reform, we have succeeded in holding greater public meetings than men have ever held for any reform. We have faced hostile mobs at street corners. If you had the power to send us to prison, not for six months but for six years, or for the whole of our lives, the Government must not think that they can stop this agitation. It will go on. We are going to win.

1 What reason does Emmeline Pankhurst give in Source 4 for their breaking the law?

2 What other messages are contained in her comment?

Source 5

▲ A drawing from the WSPU newspaper, *The Suffragette*, in 1909 showing force-feeding of a Suffragette.

Source 6

From an article in the medical journal, the *Lancet*, published in August 1912.

Prisoners were held down by force, flung on the floor, tied to chairs and iron bedsteads while the tube was forced up the nostrils. After each feeding the nasal pain gets worse.

… The wardress tried to make the prisoner open her mouth by sawing the edge of the cup along the gums, the broken edge causing cuts and severe pain.

… food into the lung of one unresisting prisoner immediately caused severe choking and vomiting. She was hurriedly released the next day suffering from pneumonia and pleurisy.

We cannot believe that any of our colleagues will agree that this form of prison treatment is justly described in Mr McKenna's words as 'necessary medical treatment'.

Hunger strikes and force-feeding

Meanwhile in prison a battle of wills was taking place between the government and Suffragettes. When Suffragettes were sent to prison the government treated them as ordinary criminals rather than as political prisoners. This meant they received harsh treatment in prison. In this way the authorities hoped to intimidate and frighten the Suffragettes. However, in response many of the women went on hunger strike. The government did not want any of the women to die as they would become martyrs and win greater sympathy. Instead, the government instructed the prisons to force-feed the women as described in Sources 5 and 6.

Truce

In January 1910 the Liberal Government promised to introduce a Conciliation Bill to give women the vote. The Suffragettes suspended militant action. But the Liberals had still not got the Bill through Parliament by the end of 1910. An angry demonstration turned to a riot on Black Friday, 18 November 1910. The government instructed police to treat the protesters firmly. Many women complained afterwards they had been violently and sexually abused by police officers. The government refused to investigate these claims.

Then, in November 1911, Asquith incensed the Suffragette leaders by announcing he was dropping plans for a women's suffrage bill to focus on a bill to extend the vote to all men! He said that women's franchise could be tacked on as an amendment. This triggered the final and most violent phase of the Suffragette campaign.

Activities

Violence chart
1 Fill out the next part of your chart, showing what happened between 1906 and 1911.
2 Discuss: do you think force-feeding was an effective tactic by the government?

131

The campaign of violence

From the end of 1911 the Suffragettes' campaign became increasingly violent. Emmeline Pankhurst said she was determined to 'create an intolerable situation for the government'. With other 'warriors' from her 'army', as she called them, the Suffragettes' policy was open lawbreaking to guarantee arrest and imprisonment.

The focus changed too. For example, previous attacks had been on government buildings. Now men's clubs and shops were targeted. Suffragettes dug up race courses and golf courses (many golf clubs were male-only clubs). They bombed and burned public buildings. Some Suffragettes developed their own tactics unknown to the WSPU leadership. Emily Davison poured chemicals into post boxes to destroy letters. 'Slasher Mary' Richardson attacked a famous painting in the National Gallery. And it was not only attacks on property. In 1912 Mary Leigh threw a small axe into Prime Minister Asquith's carriage and Gladys Evans tried to set fire to the Theatre Royal where the Prime Minister had attended a performance.

However, do not think that all the other methods of protest had ended. The Suffragettes were still producing posters and newspapers, china, badges – all in the purple, white and green of the Suffragette movement. Some Suffragettes used the tactic of tax-resistance (see Source 9).

Source 9

From the *Standard* newspaper, 1913.

No Vote No Tax

Tax-resistance is becoming more and more common amongst supporters of votes for women. It is a means of putting pressure on the Government. It also makes a strong public protest about the unfairness of women being taxed in the same way as men and yet being refused the right to vote.

The 'Cat and Mouse Act' in 1913

With hundreds of 'warriors' going to prison and on each hunger strike, the government responded with the 'Cat and Mouse Act'. The authorities could now release each hunger striker before she became too ill. When she was well again she would be re-arrested to serve the rest of her sentence. When back in prison the women once again went on hunger strike, were released, got strong, were re-arrested, went on hunger strike … and so on, like a game of cat and mouse.

Source 7

Winifred Mayo recalls her experiences of throwing stones at a men's club. (Winifred joined the Suffragette movement in 1907. Emmeline Pankhurst had asked for volunteers to go out and break windows. Some men who had been in the club attended the next Suffragette meeting to find out why Winifred had attacked their building.)

We thought it would be a good thing for a group of us to break windows of the various men's clubs. I went with a pocket full of stones and went looking for a suitable window. I didn't know which club it was and hurled a stone. To me great joy and satisfaction it broke the window. I was seized by the porter and he sent for the police. I explained the point of the attack. I was sent to prison for a fortnight.

Source 8

From *The Times*, 5 March 1912, reporting on a window smashing campaign in London.

Were it not for the calculated and determined manner in which this work of devastation was carried out one would suppose it had been wrought by demented and maniacal creatures, and even as it is a survey of the scene suggests that the mischief was done by people of unstable mental equilibrium.

June 1913: a martyr

In June 1913, Emily Davison stepped out in front of the King's horse at the Derby horse race and died five days later from her injuries. The debate continues to this day as to whether she expected to die or only intended to pin a Suffragette rosette on the King's horse and disrupt the race. Through her life Emily Davison had been regarded suspiciously by some Suffragette leaders. Her extreme actions, such as setting fire to letterboxes, were done on her own accord and were not approved by Emmeline Pankhurst. But in her death she became their martyr. The Suffragette propaganda machine sprang into action.

A memorial procession in London was followed by her funeral at Morpeth in Northumberland. These events gave Emmeline Pankhurst the greatest publicity she could have hoped for. Despite declining Suffragette membership from 1912, hundreds of Suffragettes wearing the WSPU colours – purple (dignity), white (purity) and green (hope) – marched silently next to Emily Davison's coffin.

Source 10

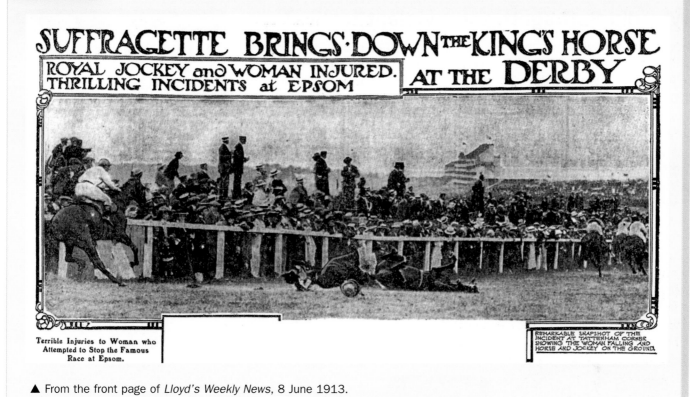

SUFFRAGETTE BRINGS·DOWN THE KING'S HORSE AT THE DERBY

ROYAL JOCKEY and WOMAN INJURED.
THRILLING INCIDENTS at EPSOM

Terrible Injuries to Woman who
Attempted to Stop the Famous
Race at Epsom.

REMARKABLE SNAPSHOT OF THE
INCIDENT AT TATTENHAM CORNER
SHOWING THE WOMAN FALLING AND
HORSE AND JOCKEY ON THE GROUND

▲ From the front page of *Lloyd's Weekly News*, 8 June 1913.

All the newspapers reported the event and the most modern form of news coverage, the newsreel cinemas, sent cameras to film the scenes too. It became one of the most remembered acts of the Suffragette movement. Even so, when Parliament debated women's suffrage in 1913, support among MPs was the lowest it had been for years!

August 1914: Suffragette campaign suspended

In August 1914 the First World War started. WSPU tactics changed completely. Protests were suspended. In return the government released all Suffragette prisoners. Emmeline Pankhurst called on her supporters to help the war effort and through their work prove they deserved the vote. Many women entered jobs which had previously been regarded as the preserve of men and made an enormous contribution.

Women win the vote!

In 1918 Prime Minister David Lloyd George, who had led the government since 1916, supported an Act through Parliament granting all women over 30 the right to vote. This was seen as an acceptable compromise and gained support from men who did not want 'foolish young women' having the vote. In 1928 a further law was passed granting all women over 21 the vote.

Activities

Violence graph
1 Fill out the next part of your graph showing what happened between 1911 and 1914.
2 Discuss: do you think that the Suffragette campaign of violence helped their cause?

Protest checklist
3 Create a Protest checklist (see page 122) to record what you need to remember about the Suffragette protest.

Factors chart
4 Make a copy of the Factor chart on page 123. Add examples of how the factors in the chart affected this protest.

Protest checklist

Why did Suffragettes use violent tactics?

In this enquiry you have been examining why Suffragette protest turned violent. Sources can help you answer this question. Sometimes the source will tell you something directly about this – for example Source 7 on page 132. But sometimes you have to infer. An **inference** is something you can work out from a source even though the source does not explicitly say it or show it.

How to ... annotate and infer from sources

When you are making inferences it will help if you annotate the source like this.

- **Step 1**: Comprehension. Label all the obvious clues in the source. Write them in the inner box.
- **Step 2**: Make inferences. What does this source suggest? Write them in the outer box.

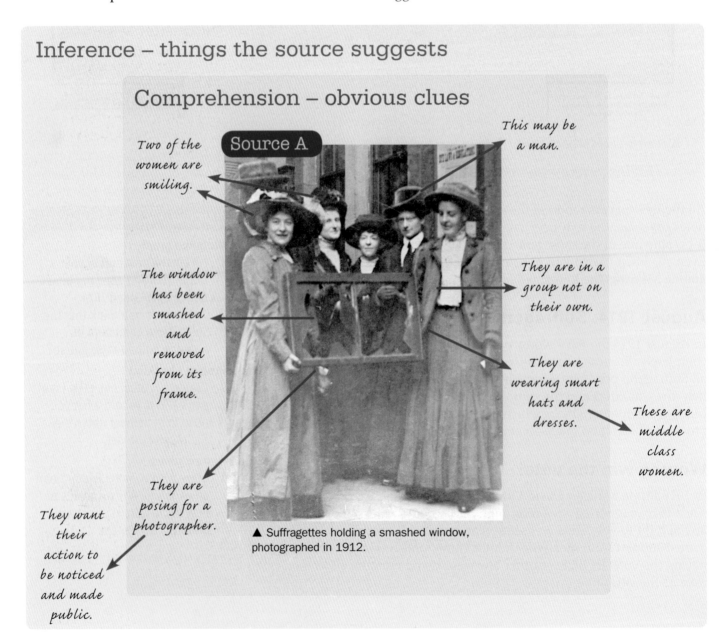

Inference – things the source suggests

Comprehension – obvious clues

Source A

This may be a man.

Two of the women are smiling.

The window has been smashed and removed from its frame.

They are in a group not on their own.

They are wearing smart hats and dresses.

These are middle class women.

They are posing for a photographer.

They want their action to be noticed and made public.

▲ Suffragettes holding a smashed window, photographed in 1912.

Answering 'inference questions' in the exam

The first question on the Source Enquiry exam paper will usually be an inference question. For example:

> What can you learn from Source A about protest methods used by Suffragette campaigners? **[6 marks]**

The Source shows Suffragettes posing with a window they have smashed. This suggests that the Suffragettes used window smashing as a deliberate tactic to draw attention to their cause. It was not because they were frustrated and could not contain themselves but because they wanted publicity. From their expressions you can see they are proud of what they have done. They might even be hoping to get arrested.

The women are dressed in smart hats and dresses ...

Activities

2 Read this student's answer (left). Note how the student **uses the key details** in Source A **to develop inferences** about protest methods used by Suffragette campaigners. Each inference is **supported by a specific reference to the source**.

3 Complete the answer with some more details and inferences.

4 Practise your skills by answering the same exam question but using Source B instead.

Source B

From *The Suffragette Movement* by Sylvia Pankhurst, a book written in 1937. Sylvia Pankhurst was one of the leaders of the WSPU, a protest movement which campaigned for women to get the vote.

On 15 December 1911 we used a new type of militant tactic. Emily Wilding Davison was arrested as she pushed a piece of linen into a post box. The linen was soaked with paraffin and burning. She had already set fire to several other post boxes and asked a police constable to arrest her. She had previously informed the press of her plans. She was tried and arrested and sentenced to six months' imprisonment.

DON'T WASTE TIME

- **Inference questions are worth only six marks** so one paragraph should be enough for full marks.

- **Stick to what you can learn from the source**. There is no need to evaluate how trustworthy the source is. You will waste valuable time and pick up no extra marks.

- **Support each inference you make with references to the source**. It is better to make two supported inferences than it is to make five or six inferences that you do not back up by referring to details in the source.

Armoured cars and soldiers on the streets of London in May 1926! Britain is not in a war. But it is in the grip of a General Strike. Nearly 3 million workers had responded to the call from the Trades Union Congress (TUC) to stop work. The unions hoped and the government feared such a strike could bring the nation to its knees. Yet within nine days the General Strike had been called off by the TUC. Why did it collapse so quickly?

Source 1

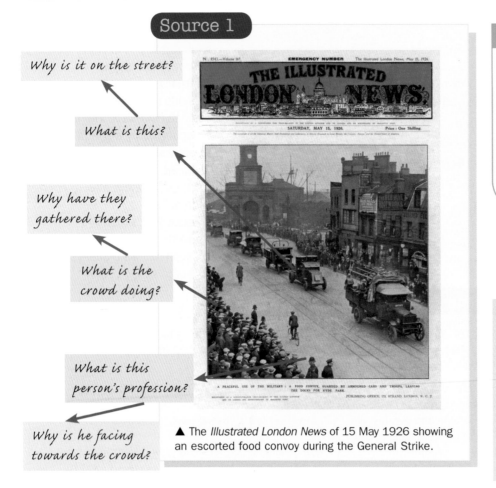

Why is it on the street?

What is this?

Why have they gathered there?

What is the crowd doing?

What is this person's profession?

Why is he facing towards the crowd?

▲ The *Illustrated London News* of 15 May 1926 showing an escorted food convoy during the General Strike.

Activity

What can you learn from Source 1 about what was happening in Britain in May 1926? Use the comprehension and inference skills you used on page 134. The annotations are there to guide you. You could use a grid as you did on page 134.

Fear of Communism

- In 1917 the Bolshevik **revolution in Russia** brought to power the world's first communist government.
- Communists believed the state should be run by the workers not by the bosses.
- The Bolsheviks also set up the **Comintern** (Communist parties of the world) **to spread revolution** to other countries.

Background to the General Strike

Fear of Socialism

- Socialism was a more moderate version of communism
- Socialists believed in state control of industry but did not want to get rid of capitalism altogether. Nor did Socialists want a violent revolution either.
- Most leaders of the powerful unions were Socialists who believed that working-class people should get more share in the profits of industries they worked in.
- To their opponents, Socialism and Communism were indistinguishable. Bosses thought that Socialism was the first step towards Communism.

Growing union power

- Union **membership** had been growing steadily.
- **Syndicalism** encouraged the creation of enormous unions from different industries.
- In Britain **the Triple Alliance** (transport, railway and miners' unions) promised to support each other if one union went on strike.
- The Trades Union Congress (TUC) was the umbrella organisation that included all the unions – although they did not directly control any of them.

Post-war economic problems

- There was an **economic slump** in Europe. **Traditional industries** such as shipbuilding, coal and textiles, which employed millions of people, were worst hit.
- To make matters worse in 1925 Britain returned to the '**gold standard**' (fixing the value of the pound to the price of gold) which made **British exports more expensive**, which created more unemployment.

How did the General Strike begin?

15 April 1921 – 'Black Friday'

- Before the First World War there had been bitter disputes between coal miners and owners.

- During the war, the coal industry was nationalised (run by the government). Wages, hours and working conditions, especially safety, all improved.

- In 1921 the coal mines were handed back to private owners who wanted to cut wages and increase working hours. The miners went on strike, expecting support from the other members of the Triple Alliance. But the Alliance felt the miners had gone on strike too quickly without negotiating and announced on 15 April 1921 that they would not support them. This day became known as 'Black Friday'. The miners were forced back to work.

31 July 1925 – 'Red Friday'

Problems in the coal industry came to the boil again in 1925. Mine owners proposed a further cut in wages and an extra hour on the working day. The miners were determined to defend their living standards. Their slogan was 'Not a penny off the pay, not a minute on the day.' Unlike 1921 other unions promised to support the miners by preventing the movement of coal. This would bring the country to a standstill – because most industries were still powered by, and most homes still heated by, coal.

The government stepped in. They agreed two measures on 'Red Friday' (31 July 1925):

- They paid the mine owners a subsidy to stop them cutting wages.

- They set up a commission led by Herbert Samuel to report on problems in the coal industry.

The miners saw this as a victory. However, while the Samuel Commission was at work, the government made detailed plans to cope if there were a general strike. They focused particularly on transport and on keeping supplies moving around the country.

March 1926 – The Samuel Report

Nine months later, in March 1926, the Samuel Report recommended that miners' hours should not increase but that miners should take a small pay cut. This was rejected by both owners and miners. Negotiations continued but the mine owners locked out the miners so they could not work. At this point the Trades Union Congress (TUC) becomes the main player. The TUC represented all the unions, not just the miners. They had the power to ask other unions to strike in support of the miners. On 27 April the TUC set up a Strike Organisation Committee to plan a national strike of key workers. It seems likely that the TUC leadership thought the threat of a strike would be enough and that talks with the government would reach a solution before it was necessary to strike. However, things came to a head much more quickly than expected.

3–4 May 1926 – The *Daily Mail*

The *Daily Mail* planned to run an article which attacked the idea of a general strike (see Source 2). The printers at the *Daily Mail* refused to print the newspaper. The government broke off negotiations with the TUC. The TUC was taken by surprise. It had no proper plans sorted out, but still ordered a strike of key workers to begin on 4 May. The General Strike had started.

> ### Source 2
>
> Part of the planned *Daily Mail* editorial, 3 May 1926.
>
> A general strike is not an industrial dispute; it is a revolutionary movement, intending to inflict suffering upon the great mass of innocent persons in the community and thus force its will upon the Government.

> ### Activity
>
> **Protest diagram: built to last?**
>
> Over the next six pages you will use a diagram like this to analyse the General Strike of 1926 and the reason why it collapsed so quickly.
>
> Discuss: which of these 'protest columns' were the strongest at the start of the General Strike?
>
> **SUCCESSFUL PROTEST depends on:**
>
> - Clear aims
> - Careful preparation
> - Personal commitment by those involved
> - Good organisation
> - Media support
> - Unity of purpose
> - Decisive leadership
> - Effective tactics

What happened during the General Strike?

Day 1: Tuesday 4 May

- As soon as the strike started, all the government's arrangements for running the country were triggered by the one word 'Action' sent by telegram. All leave for the army and navy was cancelled.
- Millions of workers from all over the country joined the strike. It was not well organised but it was extremely well supported by the Triple Alliance unions. Workers in construction, steel, electricity and printing industries also joined the first wave of the strike. Transport in London was brought to a virtual standstill.
- After a somewhat chaotic start, the Strike Organisation Committee set up by Ernest Bevin brought order, and local 'Action Councils' were set up to coordinate pickets and support the strikers.
- The public were, on the whole, good humoured about the problems caused by the strike.

Day 2: Wednesday 5 May

- Both sides published their own daily newspaper – putting their angle on events. The 'British Gazette' was published by the government. The 'British Worker' was published by the TUC.
- Attempts to run trams in London were abandoned when a large crowd formed to prevent it. Trams continued to run in most other towns. Some London buses ran with a police escort.
- Hyde Park was closed and used as a milk distribution centre by the government.

Day 3: Thursday 6 May

- Around the country 1,700 trains ran despite the railwaymen's strike, and trams and buses in many cities kept running.
- In London a few Underground trains and 80 buses ran. Some buses were attacked but the strikers were generally peaceful.
- Food convoys were given escorts of special constables, often ex-soldiers, who were resented by the strikers.
- Armed soldiers safeguarded OMS volunteers unloading ships in the docks.

Government preparations

Between July 1925 and March 1926 the government:

- set up the Organisation for the Maintenance of Supplies (OMS) to recruit volunteers to do essential jobs. There were 30,000 volunteers made up of mainly middle and upper class men, many of whom were college students. They were trained by the OMS to drive buses and lorries, and to deliver supplies in London such as milk
- divided Britain into ten regions each under a civil commissioner, with its own headquarters
- stockpiled food and fuel, including enough coal to last five months
- recruited special constables to help the police
- planned to use the armed forces to transport supplies and guard key places like docks and power stations.

- In some areas the police were very aggressive. Local strike committees set up Workers' Defence Corps to protect the pickets.

Day 4: Friday 7 May

- The government announced that a further 50,000 special constables would be recruited.
- The Archbishop of Canterbury appealed to both sides to restart negotiations but the government prevented the BBC putting out the appeal.
- 2,400 trains ran.

Day 5: Saturday 8 May

- Pickets tried to prevent lorries leaving the London docks, and so a military convoy was seen for the first time – three kilometres long with sixteen armoured cars (see Source 1 on page 136).
- Many shops and businesses that would normally be open on a Saturday remained closed.
- Prime Minister Stanley Baldwin appealed on BBC radio for the strikers to return to work.

Day 6: Sunday 9 May

- It was a quiet day. Strikers marched to church. The Archbishop of Westminster, Cardinal Bourne, called the strike 'a sin'. Some Labour MPs protested about this.
- The government appealed for more volunteers to keep order.

Day 7: Monday 10 May

- Sir Herbert Samuel tried to start negotiations with the TUC but the government said he was not acting officially.
- The 'British Gazette' claimed that a significant number of strikers were returning to work, and the government pledged to protect them from victimisation.
- The government were feeling confident that the strike would collapse. Some 3,677 trains ran.
- However, there were also signs of the strike spreading. Workers in the flour industry joined the strike. The Manchester Ship Canal was closed for the transport of wheat.

Day 8: Tuesday 11 May

- The TUC called a special meeting to discuss the progress of the strike. They asked for two more unions to join the strike: engineering and shipbuilding.

- Court action was taken by two unions (the National Sailors' Union and the Firemens' Union) to prevent the TUC calling their members out on strike. This led to a judgement by Lord Astbury that declared the strike was illegal, and that trades unions could be forced to pay compensation to employers who lost money because of the strike.
- The country was still mainly quiet but the most serious violence of the strike broke out in Glasgow. Property was damaged and there were hundreds of arrests. But, considering the size of the strike, the violence was minor.

Day 9: Wed 12 May

- At midday the TUC told the government they were calling off the strike and that they were accepting the proposal offered by Herbert Samuel. Their reason was unclear.
- Baldwin called the end of the strike a victory for common sense.
- However, rumours circulated that the government planned harsh measures: arresting TUC leaders and confiscating union funds.
- The King sent a telegram calling for an end to bitterness and no victimisation of strikers.

The TUC leadership

Leadership

Although the General Strike began because of a dispute in the mining industry the Strike was led and organised by the TUC.

The TUC set up a number of committees to run the strike. The most important was Strike Organisation Committee led by **Ernest Bevin** who was head of the Transport and General Workers Union. He was a moderate and was very suspicious of the communist tendencies of leaders such as A. J. Cook.

A. J. Cook was General Secretary of the Miners' Union. He was a Marxist who had supported syndicalism and workers' control of industry. One moderate TUC leader called him 'a raving, tearing communist'. He was a great orator, loved by the miners.

Government leaders

Government

Stanley Baldwin was Prime Minister and **Winston Churchill** was the Chancellor of the Exchequer. Both were determined to see the strike fail. Baldwin denounced the strike as 'political' and a challenge to the British constitution. Churchill, a fierce anti-communist, took a very active role, organising the OMS and editing the *British Gazette* which branded the strikers as 'the enemy' who challenged ordered government.

Activity

Look back to the Protest diagram in the Activity on page 137. Discuss:
- **a** Which of the columns seemed to be the strongest through the nine days of the General Strike?
- **b** Which were the weakest?

Battle of the media

Production of national newspapers was disrupted by the General Strike (printers were on strike) but both sides published their own. The government published the *British Gazette*, edited by Winston Churchill. It portrayed the strike as a revolutionary attempt to destroy British democracy and the rule of law.

The strikers' paper, the *British Worker*, stressed that the strike was an industrial dispute and only that. However, the newspaper was restricted to a few pages because Churchill made sure the strikers could not get enough supplies of paper to print it on.

Source 3

The British Gazette, 1926

5 May

The great strike began yesterday. There are already signs that it is by no means complete as its promoters hoped ... Volunteers came forward in large numbers in London and all the important provincial centres.

6 May

Constitutional government is being attacked. Let all good citizens whose livelihood and labour have thus been put in peril bear with fortitude and patience the hardships with which they have been so suddenly confronted ... The laws of England are the people's birthright. The laws are in your keeping. You have made Parliament their guardian. The General Strike is a challenge to Parliament and is the road to anarchy and ruin.

10 May

The work of carrying on the feeding and vital services of the population is going better every day. Nearly three thousand trains ran yesterday.

12 May

The number of individuals returning to work is increasing, and in some cases considerable groups of strikers have applied for reinstatement.

1 Look at the highlighted phrases in Sources 3 and 4. What impression does each word or phrase give of the strike?

Source 4

The British Worker, 1926

5 May

WONDERFUL RESPONSE TO CALL

The workers' response has exceeded all expectations ... they have manifested their determination and unity to the whole world ... The Trades Union General Council is not making war on the people. ... [It] wishes to emphasise the fact that this is an industrial dispute. It expects every member taking part to be exemplary in his conduct.

6 May

The workers are growing more determined as the days pass ... As to getting the 'trains and things' running with 'volunteers', the first day's boasts have quite failed to materialise. The train service remains a skeleton – and an even bonier skeleton than yesterday ... The mines are still, the goods traffic ceased, the docks are closed, the factories are closing. Not all the OMS in the world can get them going again.

11 May

STRIKE SPREADS

So far from 'dribbling back' as Mr Churchill pretends, the men on strike are standing like a rock, and more are coming out. Tomorrow another section of the Movement will be called to action.

2 Why was the government in a position to win the battle of the media?

The BBC
With the lack of newspapers, the relatively new British Broadcasting Company became important. It was the only radio broadcaster. It put out bulletins five times a day. Although supposed to be independent, it was subject to government pressure. Baldwin used it to attack the strike but neither TUC nor Labour Party leaders were allowed to broadcast. Even the Archbishop of Canterbury was not allowed to make an appeal for compromise.

Why did the TUC call off the strike so quickly?

At first, the strike enjoyed massive support. On 11 May the TUC were still trying to extend the strike to other industries. So why, on 12 May, did the TUC leadership call it off so quickly? There are a number of explanations.

- **The union movement was divided.** The TUC leadership was more moderate than the militant leaders of the miners' union. The TUC had never really wanted a general strike in the first place and had done everything they could to reach a negotiated settlement. They disliked the uncompromising attitude of A. J. Cook and did not think the miners were being realistic about conditions in the coal industry.

- **Impact on workers.** The TUC knew that the strike would cause tremendous hardship for strikers and their families who could be reduced to poverty in a short time. The longer it went on the worse it would be, and the unions would run out of funds for strike pay and be bankrupted.

- **Fear of violence.** To start with the strike was peaceful. The TUC did not think violent confrontations were the way to settle disputes. The TUC leaders were worried that the violence could escalate if the strike went on and attitudes hardened.

- **The TUC feared losing control.** In local areas strikers had set up their own 'Action Councils', organising pickets, handing out food and relieving distress. The TUC were worried about these 'Action Councils' slipping into the control of militants and communist agitators.

- **They did not want to be seen as revolutionaries.** The government put across this idea to turn the public, especially the middle classes, against the unions. The TUC leaders thought it might damage their ability to negotiate for workers in the future.

- **Little chance of winning.** The TUC leaders were realistic. Although the strike had caused major problems, supplies were getting through and it might take a long time for the strike to bite hard. They could see that the Government were determined to see out the strike and break it with every means at their disposal, including the use of the armed forces.

- **Possible compensation claims.** In a court case, a judge declared that a general strike was illegal. This opened up the possibility that unions would be liable for their employers' losses and union funds might be seized.

Activities

Look back to the Protest diagram on page 137.

1 Using the information on these two pages consider which of the columns stayed strong throughout the strike and which gave way.

2 Arrange all the reasons above into a diagram to explain why the strike collapsed so quickly. Put what you consider the most important reasons at the top and the least important at the bottom.

Protest checklist

3 Create a Protest checklist (see page 122) to record what you need to remember about the General Strike of 1926.

Factors chart

4 Find your copy of the Factors chart from page 123. Add examples of how those factors affected this protest.

The results of the General Strike

- Cook and the miners were horrified by what they saw as the TUC 'giving in' to the government. The miners refused to call off their strike. They stayed on strike for another seven months until, with funds exhausted and some families near to starvation, they accepted the owners' terms of longer hours and reduced wages.

- There was victimisation. For example, employers refused to take some workers back; demoted workers; reduced wages and/or demanded they give up trade union membership.

- The unions had lost a lot of money and union membership suffered a huge decline.

How was the General Strike portrayed?

To win the strike both sides needed to keep public support, so the way the General Strike was portrayed was an important part of the struggle. The government portrayed it as the start of a revolution, an attack on fundamental British rights and democratic government. The Labour Party and trade unions portrayed it as a fight for justice, and for a decent standard of living for working people.

How to … analyse a portrayal

Your Source Enquiry exam paper will include a question about portrayal, asking you to analyse how an artist or writer has portrayed a specific event. For example:

> What impression of the strikers is portrayed by the artist who drew Source A?
>
> **[8 marks]**

Impression this creates

These are symbols of Britain's strength

John Bull and the Union Jack

John's Bull's arms are folded.

The strikers are shown as strong but also dark and threatening.

TUC stands for Trades Union Congress who led the strike.

Comprehension – obvious clues

Source A

◀ A cartoon that appeared in *Punch* magazine on 12 May 1926.

The figure representing the strike leaders has his hand firmly on his hip.

There are factory chimneys in the distance.

The two characters have come out on to what looks like a battlefield. The environment looks devastated. The artist wants you to think that is what might happen to Britain because of the strike.

Step 1: Annotate the source – spot the obvious clues in the source

Start as you did for 'inference' questions by identifying details in the source. Write them in the inner box.

Step 2: Explain how each of these details creates a specific impression

The difference between portrayal and inference questions is that for portrayal questions the focus of your answer should be on how the artist or writer has deliberately set out to create a specific impression and put across a message. Artists and writers can create strong messages by:

- **what** they choose to include
- **how** they paint or write about it (for example through the use of colour or the use of specific words)
- using **captions**.

Answering portrayal questions in an exam

In the exam you will not be handing in an annotated source – you will have to write an explanation. Read the answer below. Notice how the student has supported each point with a specific reference to the source and then gone on to say what impression the portrayal conveys.

The cartoon shows the General Strike as an attempt to seize power. ———— Inference

The front figure is John Bull and represents the honest British ———— Reference to
people. He is standing firm with his arms folded in front of the the source
Union Jack. The impression given by the artist is that Britain will
not give in. ———— Comment on
impression/
portrayal

The other figure represents the unions who look dark and threatening ...

Activity

1 Use Steps 1 and 2 to help you analyse Source A. In the inner box label the important details. In the outer box explain what impression these create.

Activities

2 Complete the student's answer about Source A (or write your own from scratch if you think you can do better).
3 Practise your skills by analysing and writing about Source B. What impression does Source B give you of the General Strike?

Source B

From the *British Gazette*, 6 May 1926.

How London came to work
The trek to town began in the early hours of the morning, and by breakfast time a vast network of mighty traffic streams were converging on London. Motorists played the game splendidly. Some carried notices across their windscreens: 'Ask for a lift if you want one' ... Pedestrians were picked up and squeezed into cars already filled by twice the ordinary capacity. Bicycles appeared by the thousand.

WARNING

DON'T WANDER OFF THE POINT

- Portrayal questions are worth 8 marks.
- **Stick to the focus of the question**. Stick to explaining how the artist or the writer has set out to create a specific impression. There is no need to evaluate how trustworthy the source is. You will waste valuable time and pick up no extra marks.
- **Support the points you make with references to the source**. Aim to make two or three supported and developed points. Use the details in the source to support the points you make.

Case Study 3

Your enquiry

What made the miners' strike of 1984 such a bitter dispute?

Conflict in the coal industry triggered the General Strike of 1926. Sixty years later conflict between the miners and the government was still a feature of British politics. In March 1984 the longest national strike in British history began as around 100,000 coal miners began a one-year strike to protest against the planned closure of mines. This bitter dispute left its scars on mining families and communities for years to come. In this enquiry you will consider what made it such a bitter dispute.

Source 1

▲ Cartoon of Margaret Thatcher published in 1987.

Government leader: Margaret Thatcher

- British Conservative Prime Minister 1979–1990 (and first female Prime Minister)
- Renowned for her strength of character and unwillingness to back down
- Nicknamed 'the Iron Lady'
- Against state-owned industry and for capitalism
- Admired Winston Churchill.

Coal Board leader: Ian MacGregor

- Made leader of the National Coal Board (NCB) by Margaret Thatcher
- Against unions and economic waste and for efficient and profitable industry
- Had been head of the British Steel Corporation where he had cut an enormous number of jobs to make the industry more productive
- Nicknamed 'the butcher of British industry'.

Miners' leader: Arthur Scargill

- Son of a miner; a miner himself from school
- Leader of the National Union of Mineworkers (NUM) 1981–2001
- Member of the Communist Party and later the Labour Party
- Renowned as a fiery speaker and for unwillingness to compromise
- Nicknamed 'King Coal'
- Against private ownership of industry and for workers' rights
- Admired A. J. Cook, leader of the miners in the General Strike of 1926.

Background

There was a long history of conflict between coal miners and the government. You already know about this from the case study of the General Strike. But there was more recent conflict. In 1972 a miners' strike supported by other unions had put a stranglehold on the delivery of coal. This had driven the government to reduce the working week to three days to save energy and in the end the government gave in to the miners' demands for increased pay. This defeat was a major reason why the Conservatives lost the 1974 election.

The miners' aims

In the 1980s many pits were operating at a loss. The nationalised coal industry competed with cheap foreign coal and oil and gas. Demand for coal was falling. The National Union of Mineworkers (NUM) believed the government was secretly planning to close many mines. The miners wanted to keep them all open because whole communities depended on them. Arthur Scargill also strongly opposed the policies of Margaret Thatcher's government. He was ready for a fight with the government! He wanted to bring down her government in the way the miners had brought down Edward Heath's government in 1974.

The government's aims

Margaret Thatcher had become Prime Minister of a new Conservative government in 1979. She was determined to break the power of the trade unions which she thought were harming Britain's economic progress. She brought in laws to control union activity: unions had to ballot workers before a strike and unions could be fined for unlawful strikes. She also wanted to sell off the nationalised industries. She saw the coal industry as one of the worst examples: huge sums of public money subsidised inefficient mines. She had started closing mines in 1981 but stopped because of the strikes. She remembered what had happened to Heath's government in the early 1970s.

By 1984 the situation was different:

- Mrs Thatcher had led Britain to victory in the Falklands War in 1982. This had boosted her popularity. She had been re-elected in 1983. She maintained that the British people had voted for her uncompromising policies.
- She knew there was going to be a confrontation with the NUM sooner or later and had made industrial hard man Ian MacGregor head of the Coal Board.

- Britain did not depend on coal as it had in earlier times. It could import coal more cheaply than it could mine it. Power stations had been converted to run on gas or oil. Power stations had stockpiled coal in case of a miners' strike.
- Mrs Thatcher was ready for a fight with the unions!

The trigger

In March 1984 the National Coal Board (NCB) announced that Cortonwood colliery (coal mine together with its physical plants and outbuildings) near Barnsley was to be closed. Miners from all over Yorkshire went on strike. The NCB then announced a programme of twenty further pit closures resulting in 20,000 miners losing their jobs. Scottish miners joined the action and by 12 March around half of Britain's 187,000 miners were on strike.

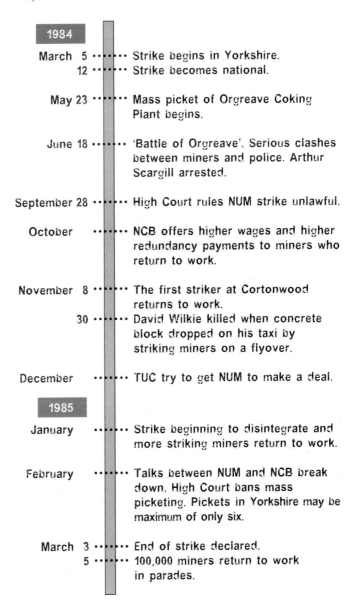

1984

March 5 ······ Strike begins in Yorkshire.
12 ······ Strike becomes national.

May 23 ······ Mass picket of Orgreave Coking Plant begins.

June 18 ······ 'Battle of Orgreave'. Serious clashes between miners and police. Arthur Scargill arrested.

September 28 ······ High Court rules NUM strike unlawful.

October ······ NCB offers higher wages and higher redundancy payments to miners who return to work.

November 8 ······ The first striker at Cortonwood returns to work.
30 ······ David Wilkie killed when concrete block dropped on his taxi by striking miners on a flyover.

December ······ TUC try to get NUM to make a deal.

1985

January ······ Strike beginning to disintegrate and more striking miners return to work.

February ······ Talks between NUM and NCB break down. High Court bans mass picketing. Pickets in Yorkshire may be maximum of only six.

March 3 ······ End of strike declared.
5 ······ 100,000 miners return to work in parades.

The miners' tactics

Arthur Scargill and the NUM knew that in order for the strike to succeed they had to bring out all the miners to completely stop the production of coal. But the NUM had not held a national ballot to see if a majority of its miners would vote for a strike. It relied on regional ballots. In some areas, particularly in Nottinghamshire and Leicestershire where the mines were not threatened with closure, they voted not to join the strike. Even in Yorkshire some mines remained open. So the NUM's tactics were focused on 'persuading' other miners to stop work.

Activity

Using these two pages add more branches to your 'bitterness' mind map for:

c   The tactics of the miners and the government

d   Other unions.

▼ Police and pickets at a Yorkshire mine, 1984

Picketing

- Mass pickets (hundreds of men) were used to block the entrances to collieries (coal mines together with their physical plants and outbuildings) to stop workers going into work and prevent coal being produced or moved. There were often violent clashes with the police, with bricks and bottles being thrown.
- 'Flying pickets', strikers brought in from other areas, were used to increase the number of pickets at any one mine, so sometimes hundreds of miners from Yorkshire flooded down to Nottinghamshire mines.

Intimidation

- Miners used the term 'scab' to describe a strike breaker. They would try to intimidate workers crossing the picket line. Non-striking miners were excluded from their community and threatened with violence.
- In mining communities the property of some non-striking miners was damaged – their gardens dug up, cars vandalised and daubed with paint. There were often confrontations between striking and working miners, and even splits within families.

Supporting striking miners

- Fundraising and advertising campaigns using posters and badges helped raise funds for the striking families.
- Women were a major force in the strike. Women in mining communities organised themselves into action groups, providing shelters, food parcels and children's events.
- One group, Women Against Pit Closures, went further and took an active part in supporting miners' pickets and going on demonstrations.
- A strike fund from the NUM allowed miners to receive some income when they were striking.

The unions and the Labour Party

- Some unions supported the strike but key ones such as the Steelworkers Union did not.
- The TUC leadership offered support but were not completely behind the strike. They did not like Scargill or his uncompromising stance which they thought was unreasonable.

The authorities' tactics

The government was determined not to be defeated by the miners as the Heath government had been in 1974, so it was important to keep the working mines open, and keep the power stations supplied with fuel. The government needed to support miners who wanted to work, so as to keep public support on their side.

Planning for the strike

- The power stations had stockpiled coal prior to the strike and built coal-to-oil convertors to keep the power stations running if the coal ran out.

Media campaign

- Mrs Thatcher made speeches condemning intimidation and bullying.
- The newspapers carried stories of miners who wanted to work and were being bullied by their union leaders and striking miners.

Source 2

Margaret Thatcher, 19 July 1984, in the House of Commons.

We had to fight the enemy without in the Falklands. We always have to be aware of the enemy within, which is much more difficult to fight and more dangerous to liberty.

Withdrawing support

- The government cut the benefits for striking miners because the strike was deemed illegal. Families received some Social Security payments but these were very small. This meant that there was very real hardship and suffering in mining communities. Miners' families lived on hand-outs, donations from the public and a small amount of strike pay.
- In October the NCB offered cash payments to miners who returned with special bonuses if they worked the four weeks before Christmas.
- The High Court ruled that the strike was illegal because the NUM had not held a ballot. When the NUM refused to pay a fine of £200,000 the Court ordered that its funds should be seized. This meant it did not have money to carry on the strike or to support strikers.

Anti-picketing

- Police officers were drafted in from across the country to create a huge police presence in the affected areas. They confronted the miners, using police horses and baton charges.
- Police prevented 'flying pickets' travelling to their destination. They stopped cars on roads and forced them to turn around.
- Later, the High Court banned mass pickets.

- The Labour Party leadership did not support the strike because a ballot had not been held, though individual Labour MPs were behind the miners.
- Neither the TUC nor the Labour Party wanted to be associated with the violence of the mass pickets and the intimidation of working miners.

Nottinghamshire miners

- The Nottinghamshire miners resolutely opposed the strike. They wanted a national ballot and objected to Scargill's manipulative methods. They were extremely angry at the arrival of scores of Yorkshire pickets in their communities, the intimidation and threats, and the damage done to their property. This probably strengthened their anti-strike stance. Later on they formed their own breakaway union, the Union of Democratic Mineworkers.

How was the miners' strike portrayed by the media?

The miners' strike dominated news headlines. Television crews and newspaper reporters were on the scene for picket line clashes between police and miners. Popular newspapers such as the *Sun* and the *Daily Mail* were very anti-strike. Television cameras and photographers were usually behind police lines, not with the miners. The miners complained that they were unfairly represented and that police taunting and violence towards them was not shown. The media reported the hardship facing miners' families but they also reported on the intimidation of working miners.

The 'Battle of Orgreave'

One of the most violent confrontations took place outside the Orgreave coking works in South Yorkshire. It was just like a battle. Pickets trying to prevent lorries delivering coal were met by police in riot gear who, along with mounted police, charged the miners. Media reports maintained that the miners had hurled bricks and bottles at the police first but this was later shown not to be true and twice as many miners were injured as police. But the miners were blamed for the violence and this went down badly with the public. Unions and Labour MPs also criticised the strikers' behaviour.

A ▲ A police officer and miner confront each other on a picket line during the strike of 1984.

B ▲ Police officers and a striking miner share a joke on the picket line just seconds after the photo above.

◄ Photographer Lesley Boulton at Orgreave. She was attending an injured miner. She was pulled out of the way by a friend just before the truncheon could hit her head. See also Source C on page 151.

The end of the strike

By Christmas 1984 many mining families were at breaking point. There was little money. Children went without presents and families without Christmas dinner. In January an increasing number of miners returned to work and the NUM could see that the strike might disintegrate. In the end the miners voted to return to work together rather than be forced back in dribs and drabs. On 5 March 1985 approximately 100,000 coal miners returned to work after a year on strike. Many went back in procession behind colliery and union banners, cheered by their communities. It was a display of strength and solidarity but they had achieved none of their aims.

Legacy: the miners

- Cortonwood Colliery (where the strike started) closed and many other pits followed.
- Because of the strike other pits had become unworkable due to flooding.
- Mass unemployment affected mining areas for decades.
- The membership of the NUM fell enormously.
- The dispute left deep hatred towards the police in the mining areas, particularly towards the Metropolitan Police who, the miners felt, had been extremely provocative and violent.
- People on different sides of the strike in the same communities still do not speak to each other.

Legacy: Mrs Thatcher

- Union power was weakened. Mrs Thatcher claimed to have 'tamed the trade unions'.
- Mrs Thatcher's victory may have won respect but some sections of the population remained hugely opposed to her. She was to feel the full force of this in the Poll Tax protests of 1990s which you will investigate in the next case study.

Activities

1 How does the portrayal in Source 3A differ from that in Source 3B?
2 Newspapers chose to use Source 3A but not Source 3B. What effect might this have on the public's perception of the miners and police?
3 How might it influence the public view of the miners' strike if most photographs and film were taken from the police side of the picket lines?

Source 5

The NUM President, Arthur Scargill, speaking to a news conference on the day the strike was called off.

We have decided to go back for a whole range of reasons. One of the reasons is that the trade union movement of Britain with a few notable exceptions has left this union isolated. Another reason is that we face not an employer but a government aided and abetted by the judiciary, the police and you people in the media and at the end of this time our people are suffering tremendous hardship.

1 Who does Arthur Scargill blame for the mines' defeat in Source 5?
2 Do you agree with his verdict? If not, what other factors has he missed?

Activities

4 Use these two pages to add two more branches to your 'bitterness' mind map for:
  e The role of the media
  f The impact of the strike on mining communities.
5 Compare your mind map with a partner's then choose one aspect of the strike that you think was particularly important in causing bitterness. Write a paragraph to explain how and why it led to such bitterness.

Protest checklist
6 Create a Protest checklist (see page 122) to record what you need to remember about the miners' strike of 1984.

Factors chart
7 Find your copy of the Factors chart from page 123. Add examples of how those factors affected this protest.

Meet the Examiner: 'Cross-reference' questions

Do the sources agree about the miners' strike?

When you study a topic as bitter as the miners strike you expect to find lots of disagreements between the sources. You will be unlikely to find a single source that explains events from both sides. To get a more accurate picture of the strike you need to compare sources. This skill is known as **cross-referencing.**

 ## How to ... cross-reference sources

	Source A	Source B
Step 1: Key ideas or details		
Step 2: Overall message		
Step 3: Provenance		

You can use a chart like this to compare two sources.

Step 1: Record key ideas or details

… then compare these details to see if they agree or disagree.

Step 2: Establish the overall message of each source

Many students compare the details in each source but do not look at the overall message of each source. It is important to establish if the overall message is different in both sources.

Step 3: Evaluate the provenance

Cross-referencing is not only about what the source says but about who wrote it and why. Is there any reason to trust one source more than the other because of its provenance?

Step 4: Think carefully about the extent to which one source supports or challenges another source

Does Source A totally contradict Source B? Look carefully again at the key messages in each source and the provenance.

Source A

Extracts from a BBC interview with the Chief Constable (CC) of South Yorkshire police after the 'Battle of Orgreave'.

BBC: There has been violence on picket lines before. Was the violence more serious this time?

C C: Well it would appear so. I've not known that missiles have been thrown to the extent that they have here. It may well be that the location and the nature of the ground allows stones to be thrown and the pickets run away and that is the concern that I have that the pickets have free range to throw at my officers and my officers are suffering injury.

BBC: Have you not considered that if there was a lower police presence then perhaps the violence would not be as great?

C C: We keep the police presence in accordance with the number of pickets. If there is a small number of pickets there is a small police presence. There has been a regular official picket on the gate of that plant and that picket has spoken to the drivers daily. Mr Scargill has been in and spoken to the drivers and they have indicated that they want the right to go in and out of that coal plant and they want protection and it's my job at this stage to do exactly that.

Source B

Arthur Scargill speaking after the 'Battle of Orgreave'.

We've had riot shields, we've had riot gear, we've had police on horseback charging into our people, we've had people hit with truncheons and people kicked to the ground …The intimidation and the brutality displayed are sometimes reminiscent of a Latin American state.

Activity

1 Use Steps 1–4 to compare what Sources A and B say about the 'Battle of Orgreave'.

Answering cross-reference questions in the exam

In your Source Enquiry you will be asked to compare the message in two sources. For example:

> To what extent does Source A challenge the view of police tactics given in Source B? **[10 marks]**

Writing your answer – make direct comparisons

Some students answer this type of question poorly because they waste time describing what each source says before they begin to answer the question. Avoid lengthy descriptions of the source. Instead focus on analysing the differences or similarities. The best answers make **direct comparisons** between the two sources throughout.

Activity

2 Practise your cross-reference skills on Source C. How far does Source C challenge or confirm the views in Sources A and B?

Paragraph 1: Explain how Source A challenges Source B.

> *Source B gives the impression that …*
> *However, Source A suggests that …*

Paragraph 2: Explain ways in which Source A does not challenge Source B.

> *Source A does not challenge all the messages given in Source B. For example …*

Paragraph 3: Comment on the provenance or origins of each source and how that strengthens or weakens the challenge.

> *Source A is a spoken interview so …*

Paragraph 4: Reach an overall judgement about the extent to which Source A challenges Source B.

> *Overall, Source A challenges Source B to a large/small extent. This is because …*

Source C

From a radio interview (I) with Lesley (L) Boulton (the woman seen in Source 4 on page 148).

L: You got the sense that they [the police] were just out of control and quite a few miners were injured on the day. One young lad that I took a photo of had his leg broken. There were quite a lot of injuries.

I: If the policeman's baton had hit you, would it probably have knocked you out?

L: Oh absolutely, without equivocation.

I: Do you think the policeman thought you were a miner?

L: I don't know, I was holding a camera as I was trying to attract attention and I don't know what he thought really. The police were completely carried away. Some of them were laughing and obviously enjoying this exercise of their power.

DON'T WRITE LONG DESCRIPTIONS

✓ Plan your approach to cross-referencing questions carefully.

✗ Do not go through everything that Source A tells you, then everything Source B tells you and leave it to the examiner to pull out the similarities and differences!

✓ Instead make direct comparisons as you go through your answer.

Case Study 4

Your enquiry
Why was the Poll Tax protest successful in achieving its aims?

Five years after the miners were defeated by Margaret Thatcher's government, Thatcher herself was brought down by a protest led by ordinary people. What was different this time? Why did the Poll Tax protest succeed?

Activity

At the end of this enquiry you are going to consider why the Poll Tax protest succeeded. Over pages 152–157 you will make notes. Make notes from these two pages under these two headings:
- why people thought the poll tax was unfair
- who was involved in the protest.

What was the Poll Tax?

Local government helps pay for local services by collecting local taxes. Before 1990 these were called 'rates' and were based on the size of the house you lived in. Rates were not related directly to how rich you were, but usually the more money you had, the bigger your house, so there was often a link between what you paid in rates and how wealthy you were. However, the system had been introduced back in the nineteenth century and most people agreed it needed reforming. But how?

The Conservative government led by Margaret Thatcher decided on a very controversial alternative. They introduced what they called a 'Community Charge' – every employed adult would pay the same charge whatever they earned. It was dubbed the Poll Tax (because everyone on the electoral roll would have to pay it). Pensioners would pay 25 per cent of the charge; students and the unemployed 20 per cent. It was up to each council to decide on the level of charge, but within that authority every employed adult would then pay the same.

Why was it introduced?

Mrs Thatcher criticised rates because the people who used the fewest services paid the most tax. She believed the opposite should be true. She explained the Poll Tax in her memoirs: 'Anyone who could reasonably afford to do so should at least pay something towards the services from which they benefited. A whole class of people – an "underclass" if you will – had been dragged back into the ranks of responsible society and asked to become not just dependents but citizens.' Underlying all this was the Conservative attempt to make local councils spend less money.

Why was it so unpopular?

All taxes are unpopular and governments have to be very careful how they introduce them. This new tax was deeply unpopular. The fairest taxes are 'progressive' – people pay more if they earn more. The Poll Tax was 'regressive' – the poor ended up paying proportionately more than the rich. It was estimated that the Prime Minister herself would end up paying £2,300 *less* per year, while a typical family in Suffolk, say, would end up paying £640 *more*.

People who would **gain** from the poll tax	People who would **lose** from the poll tax
People with big houses. The Poll Tax would be lower than their rates.	People in rented accomodation or small houses with low rateable value. The Poll Tax would be higher than their rates.
Pensioners who had previously paid rates. Pensioners had to pay only 25% of the tax.	People on benefits who never had to pay rates but now had to pay 20% of the Community Charge.
People living alone as they had to pay only one tax.	Households with over-18s living at home as everyone in the family had to pay.

Poll Tax protest – timeline

1986

January .... Conservative government publish plans to replace rates with the 'Community Charge' or Poll Tax.

1987

April .... First Anti-Poll Tax Union (APTU) set up in Maryhill, Glasgow

June .... Mrs Thatcher comfortably wins third election. She announces Poll Tax is a 'flagship policy' of her new government

December .... First Anti Poll-Tax Federation set up in Scotland to coordinate local APTUs

1989

July .... Poll Tax introduced in Scotland

APTUs established across the country; 25% of Scots refuse to pay the tax

25 November .... 2,000 delegates from 1,000 APTUs gather at meeting to plan resistance to the Poll Tax

November .... Large anti-Poll Tax meetings all over the country. 2,000 attend an anti-Poll Tax meeting in Maidenhead (a very Conservative area)

1990

31 March .... Mass protest in London
1 April .... Poll Tax introduced in England and Wales

May .... Conservatives do badly in local elections in England

June .... Courts in Isle of Wight throw out 1,800 prosecutions of Poll Tax refusers.

August .... An estimated 20% of the population had not paid any Poll Tax four months after its introduction

22 November .... Margaret Thatcher resigns

1991

April .... Prime Minister John Major announces abandonment of the Poll Tax.

1993

.... Poll Tax finally abolished – by which time an estimated 18 million people have refused to pay. It is replaced by Council Tax, based on the market value of a person's property.

Protesters gather in London for a demonstration ▶ against the Poll Tax. There were 200,000 protesters – far beyond the organisers' expectations.

Who was against the Poll Tax?

The key thing to realise is that **all sorts of different people objected to the Poll Tax and joined the protest for different reasons.**

- Far-left groups such as Militant (whose members had been ejected from the Labour Party for being too extreme) saw this as an opportunity to get working class people involved in politics and challenging the government.

- Many ordinary people such as students opposed it because they found they would have to pay more tax.

- Some richer people opposed it on principle – even if they would pay less tax themselves. They still thought it was wrong for the rich to pay the same amount of tax as the poor.

- Thatcher's policies in the previous eight years had earned her many enemies, particularly in the anti-union period of the 1980s when she took on the miners. Now all her enemies, who might not agree on anything else, could unite around this single cause. It was not only anti-Poll Tax feeling but also anti-Thatcher feeling.

How did people protest against the Poll Tax?

The timeline on the previous page summarises the main events of the Poll Tax protest. The main drivers of the protest were over 1,000 local Anti-Poll-Tax Unions (APTUs) around the country. Their tactics included:

- **Non-payment** – encouraging people not to pay and supporting them in facing the consequences, for example in resisting bailiffs (people who take your property when you have failed to pay someone). Non-payment was illegal. You could be sent to prison for it. But non-payment was very common. Around one in five people had not made a payment by August 1990

- **Protest meetings and marches** which usually ended in a protest outside the local council offices. Lambeth Council called in riot police to protect them against angry protesters when the councillors met to agree the level of the Poll Tax

- **Political debate and lobbying** – for example, meeting MPs or writing letters

- **Making leaflets, badges, stickers and posters** such as Source 1

- **Persuading councils not to implement the Poll Tax** or not to prosecute non-payers. Although there were many people in local councils who claimed to be against the Poll Tax they were not prepared to go against the government and risk punishment, so this policy did not really succeed.

To pay or not to pay?

The big issue was whether to support non-payment (see Sources 1–3). The APTUs were set up to support non-payment but Thatcher's political opponents, such as the Labour Party, were not prepared to back this policy. The Poll Tax was a law passed by Parliament. They did not think they could back a campaign to encourage people to break the law.

Source 1

▲ An early anti-Poll Tax badge from 1989.

Source 2

Peter Taaffe writing in *Militant* magazine, 12 February 1988.

The vast majority [of British people] are opposed to the tax, but the Labour leaders have made it clear that the struggle is to be restricted to Parliament. But the history of this government is that they do not listen to parliamentary speeches. Only when a mass struggle is mobilised can the labour movement force the 'Iron Lady' to retreat. There is an explosive situation developing on the housing estates. The Government has made a big error.

Source 3

Part of Christine McVicar's speech in October 1989 when she tore up her Poll Tax payment book at the Labour Party conference. This was shown in TV news bulletins. She had called on the Labour Party to back the policy of non-payment.

Without the Tolpuddle trade unionists and the Suffragettes breaking the law, we wouldn't be here at this conference ... I'm ripping up my Poll Tax book not as an individual but as part of a mass campaign of non-payment.

31 March 1990: The London riots

On 31 March 1990 a national protest march took place in London, the day before the introduction of the tax in England and Wales. The police had expected 60,000 protesters, but in reality up to 200,000 came. Two feeder marches followed the routes of the Peasants' Revolt of 1381.

The day began peacefully with families and friends gathering in London parks and marching through the capital. They headed for Trafalgar Square where politicians and campaigners would speak to the crowd.

Not all the marchers could fit in Trafalgar Square so they were in surrounding streets. One group of protesters headed towards Downing Street (off the agreed route of the march) and fights broke out when the police tried to move them on. Violence then spread. More police arrived dressed in riot gear. Peaceful bystanders got caught up in the violence. Some protesters armed themselves with scaffolding and bricks and began to vandalise nearby buildings. Buildings and cars were set on fire, shops were looted (see Source A on page 158). There were 400 arrests, 113 injuries (including 45 police), and the cost of damage was estimated to be £400,000.

Some blamed the protesters for the violence – others blamed the police. You can find out more about this protest on page 158.

Source 5

An anti-Poll Tax protester's eyewitness account written after the event for a workers' magazine.

I continued with the crowd, marching up Northumberland Avenue (towards Trafalgar Square). It became apparent that something had already started. A man was fighting his way back through the crowd. A real sense of panic hit me as I heard him shouting, 'Get any kids out of the way, they're going to charge!' Images sped through my mind of the mothers with young kids, old people, disabled people that I had seen on the march. They were all here in the Square, the police were going to charge us and there was no way out! Bloodbath! As I looked up the length of the road, I saw a police van speeding towards us and it screeched to a halt as an unsuspecting body flew through the air on impact and landed in a heap on the side of the road.

Source 4

David Meynell, Deputy Assistant Commissioner of the Metropolitan Police, who was in charge of the police operation, interviewed for television soon after 31 March.

A peaceful march was completely overshadowed by the actions of about 3,000 to 3,500 people in minority groups who without any doubt at all launched a ferocious and sustained attack on the police.

What was the impact of the London protest?

The London riot could have been a disaster for the anti-Poll Tax movement. The government said events showed the movement was in the hands of extremists. Newspapers condemned the violent protesters. The *Sun* newspaper even went so far as to print pictures of protesters wanted by the police. But the media also sympathised with the innocent public caught up in the chaos – news cameras had filmed police brutality and, unlike the miners' strike, this time such images were televised. For most people the sight of such awful violence on the streets of the capital city made them afraid of what might happen next, and more determined to solve the problem that was causing this – the Poll Tax. The writer Robert Harris commented in the *Sunday Times* newspaper: 'I doubt whether the ordinary voter, watching the violence on television, says: "Look at those horrible communists, Mabel. We must vote for Mrs Thatcher as the only person who can deliver us from these ruffians." The voter is more likely to say: "Look at the latest bloody mess that woman has landed us in."'

Activity

At the end of this enquiry you are going to consider why the Poll Tax protest succeeded. Make notes from these pages under these two headings:
- the methods of protest used by the protesters
- the impact of the riots on 31 March 1990.

Why was the Poll Tax abolished?

The Poll Tax was formally introduced in England and Wales the day after the London protest. It soon became clear how successful the non-payment campaign was. Four months after its introduction an estimated 20 per cent of people around the country were refusing to pay the tax. In cities the numbers of non-payers were much higher – in some areas of London over 50 per cent refused to pay.

The lost revenue was damaging local councils. Chasing non-payment and prosecuting offenders was costly, ineffective and unpopular. It required taking the non-payer to court, then seizing their property. In June the courts in the Isle of Wight abandoned prosecutions of 1,800 Poll Tax refusers. It would have been a waste of time and money to prosecute so many people.

It was clear that if the Poll Tax were to continue, Margaret Thatcher would be fighting the biggest battle of her career. In the miners' strike she had had the majority of the country on her side in tackling union power. In this battle she was fighting millions of ordinary Britons – including many who had previously been her staunchest supporters. One commentator said: 'I knew that Thatcher was done for when I read that according to official figures a third of the people of Tunbridge Wells aren't paying.'

In the May local elections the Conservatives had fared badly, losing control of many councils. The implications for the Conservative party were clear to many MPs – this unpopular policy could lose them the next general election. Thatcher was not going to do a U-turn on the tax – she had made it her central policy – so she was challenged for the leadership of her party. When it was clear she was not going to win, she resigned. The Poll Tax was not the only issue that dislodged her, but it was the key reason why her reputation in the party had fallen. A few months later, in April 1991, the new Prime Minister, John Major, announced that the Poll Tax would be abolished.

The protestors had defeated the government on a single issue – that of taxation. This was unprecedented in the twentieth century. No previous protest had so publicly challenged and defeated a government in this way.

Activities

Why did the Poll Tax protest succeed?

1   In this enquiry you are considering why the Poll Tax protest succeeded. Make notes from these pages under these two headings:
    - the effect of non-payment
    - the reasons why Margaret Thatcher resigned.

Writing up your conclusions

2   Below are five factors which help to explain why the protest succeeded. Choose the ones that you think are most important and write a paragraph to explain your choice. Use the notes you have made through the enquiry to support your answer with evidence.
    - The unfairness of the tax
    - The difficulties councils had in collecting the tax
    - Margaret Thatcher's character and actions
    - Actions of ordinary people
    - The London riots of March 1990.

Protest checklist

3   Create a new Protest checklist (see page 122) to record what you need to remember about the Poll Tax protest.

Factors chart

4   Find your copy of the Factors chart from page 123. Add examples of how those factors affected this protest.

Source 6

From *British Government in Crisis*, by Christopher D. Foster, 2005.

[the disaster was caused by] ...the political will of the Prime Minister, which prevented searching discussion of the issues and swamped civil service advice on the difficulties to be overcome ... After Thatcher had decided on the Poll Tax neither its fairness nor collectability could be got sufficiently on the agenda for solutions to be reached.

Source 7

◄ 'The Evolution Of The Iron Lady', from the *Economist*, November 1990.

Activities

5 Source 7 (above) is to appear in a museum about twentieth century history. Using what you have found out from the last two case studies (the Miners' Strike and the Poll Tax protest), write a 200-word caption to explain what it shows.

Judgement time!

6 You have now completed your four Protest case studies. Some protests succeeded, some failed. And there was a range of factors that determined their success or failure. Use your Protest checklists and your Factors chart to help you.

a Choose one case study that you think fits into each of these categories:
- A protest that was undermined by bad leadership
- A protest that was really well organised but still failed
- A protest where the media played a crucial role in supporting or undermining it
- A protest that had popular support
- A protest where the authorities were criticised for how they handled it.

b Choose one example only. Write a paragraph to explain your choice and support your answer with evidence from this book or your own research.

Meet the Examiner: 'Usefulness' questions

Which are the most useful sources for finding out about the Poll Tax protests?

One of the most famous events of the Poll Tax protests was the London march on 31 March 1990 that led to rioting. With nearly 200,000 people on the march there were lots of eyewitnesses and many have written about their experiences. There were also many TV cameras and photographers at the event so there are many hours of film and thousands of photos. There were dozens of influential political leaders involved. And after the event the police conducted enquiries into what had happened, so there is a mass of evidence about this event. When a historian is faced by so many sources one of the most important things is to select the most useful sources. Usefulness depends on purpose. Sources are never useful or useless in their own right. It all depends on what you are using them for.

For example, say we are investigating why the Poll Tax march turned violent and specifically whether police tactics were to blame. How would these two sources be useful?

Source B

A photographer who was independently shooting pictures on the scene recollects the events of 31 March for a *Socialist Worker*'s pamphlet published in June 1990. The Socialist Workers' Party (SWP), a far left group, were involved in organising the campaigns of non-payment.

More than 100,000 people of all ages marched from Kennington Park in South London to Trafalgar Square to hear various speakers. Initially the march was peaceful and good-humoured. But a small group near the tail of the march staged a sit-down protest outside Downing Street. As the police started to move them on scuffles developed and the first arrests were made. As the riot escalated in size and violence the first police were injured. The police tactics used to quell the riot were the subject of some controversy. Some rioters broke into a construction site overlooking Trafalgar Square and set fire to it. Others went on looting sprees.

Source A

▲ Police and demonstrators clash in Trafalgar Square on 31 March 1990. This image appeared in many newspapers the day after.

How to ... evaluate the usefulness of sources

Step 1: Consider the *content* of both sources

- What does each source tell you that would be useful in your enquiry? Use your inference skills as well: what can you work out from the source that would be useful?
- Most sources will have limitations too. Think about what is missing from the source. What does it *not* tell you that you need to know?

Step 2: Consider the *provenance* of both sources

Read the caption which will tell you more about the source.

- What type of source is it?
- Who wrote or produced it?
- When?
- Why was it produced?
- How typical is it?
- And most importantly: how do the answers to the questions above increase or reduce the reliability and usefulness of the source?

Step 3: Reach an overall judgement

Always end with a conclusion in which you reach a judgement as to which source is most useful and why.

- **How** useful is each source (very/quite)?
- Which source is the **more** useful? (Don't sit on the fence – reach a judgement and back it up)
- What is your **key reason** for reaching this judgement?

You can use a chart like this to help you.

	Source A	Source B
Step 1: Content		
Step 2: Provenance		
Step 3: Overall judgement		

Answering 'usefulness' questions in an exam

Here is an example of a 'usefulness' question that you might find in an exam.

> Study Sources A and B. Which is more useful to the historian who is investigating the role of the police in the Poll Tax Riot of 31 March 1990? Explain your answer referring to Sources A and B. **[10 marks]**

This question requires you to evaluate how far the information in each source would help the historian in understanding the role of police. Here is a plan.

Paragraph 1: Comment on the content of each source.

Source A is useful because it helps us understand ...
We also learn that ...
However, Source A has some limitations. It does not
provide us with information on ... or evidence of ...

Now do the same for Source B.

Paragraph 2: Comment on the content of each source.

Source B is a ...
The advantage of this is ...

Now do the same for Source A.

Paragraph 3: Summarising your overall judgement.

Be positive:

You need to consider the strengths **and** weaknesses of a source. However ... the question is asking you how **useful** the sources are, not how **useless** they are. There will not be any sources that are completely useless. Don't get bogged down telling the examiner what is wrong with the source.

Analyse, don't repeat

Don't fall into the trap of repeating what the source says in your own words. Explain how the source can be used. Explain why it contains useful information.

Information is not the same as usefulness

Remember that the usefulness of a source is not about how much information it contains. It is whether or not it helps you answer the question that you are investigating.

159

The final question of your exam will ask you to use the sources and your own knowledge to reach a judgement. For example:

> **5** Study Sources C, G and H.
>
> 'The General Strike failed because the authorities were more organised than the unions and strikers.' How far do you agree with this statement? Use your own knowledge, Sources C, G and H, and any other sources you find helpful. **[16 marks]**

Step 1: Decode the question

The examiners are not trying to catch you out: they are giving you a chance to show what you know – **and what you can do with what you know**. If you work out what the question is asking for, you will be able to answer if from what you have learned.

You need to read an exam question more than once. If you do not do this you could miss the point and miss out on lots of marks. Aim to spot the following four key features of a question. You could use a different colour for each.

1 **Date boundaries** – What time period should you cover in your answer? Stick to this carefully otherwise you will waste time writing about events that are not relevant to the question.

2 **Content focus** – The topic the examiner wants you to focus on.

3 **Question type** – Different question types require different approaches. Look for key words like *'what'*, *'why'*, or *'how far'* that will help you work out what type of approach is needed.

4 **Marks available** – Look at how many marks the question is worth. This gives you a guide as to how much you are expected to write and how much time to allocate. Do not spend too long on questions that are only worth a few marks.

The question mentions organisation but this question is not just about organisation. It throws you one possible reason for failure but you have to weigh that against the other reasons you have examined such as the role of the media; or the divisions within the union movement.

This question does not have any date boundaries but sometimes it will, particularly if you are studying one of the longer protests such as the Suffragettes when things changed a lot over time. So stick to what they ask you. That will help you stay relevant to the question.

> **5** Study Sources C, G and H.
>
> 'The General Strike failed because the authorities were more organised than the unions and strikers.'
> How far do you agree with this statement?
> Use your own knowledge, Sources C, G and H, and any other sources you find helpful. **[16 marks]**

The question asks you to <u>evaluate</u> the statement. Don't jump to a conclusion. You need to explore evidence that supports and evidence that challenges the statement before coming to a conclusion. Then in your final paragraph you will be able to state how far you agree with the statement.

Sixteen marks are available, more marks than any other question in the exam paper, so you need to produce a carefully planned and detailed answer. A short paragraph or a quick list of points will not get you many marks!

Step 2: Plan your approach to the question

At this point you have already reached your own opinion on the question. However it is not simply a case of saying whether you agree or disagree with the statement; 16 marks are available so the examiner will expect you to **explore both sides of the argument** before you reach a conclusion.

You should write three paragraphs:

- Paragraph 1 should explore **the evidence that supports** the statement. Why might the authorities have been seen to be more organised than the unions and strikers? Use the sources and your own knowledge to show how the General Strike failed due to lack of organisation among the unions and strikers.

- Paragraph 2 should explore **evidence against** the statement. What evidence could you use from the sources and your own knowledge to argue against the statement?

- Paragraph 3 is your **conclusion**. You need to reach an overall judgement. To what extent do you agree or disagree with the statement? Remember to explain your thinking.

Step 3: Use connectives to tie what you know to the question

Always back up your statements with evidence to prove your arguments. Any general point needs to be fully explained and backed up with specific examples from your own knowledge AND the sources.

Step 4: Use the sources to support your answer

This is a source enquiry. So you must base your answer in the sources on the exam paper. You will not achieve a good grade if you ignore the sources and simply write an answer to this final question based on your own knowledge. You should use both your knowledge and the sources.

- You must use the sources specified in the questions.
- You can use any other sources you wish.
- You do not have to use all the sources.
- Make sure you refer to a source by letter/number so that the examiner can see which source you are using to support your answer.
- Wherever possible, try to group sources together rather than going through each source in turn.

Step 5: Think carefully about your concluding paragraph

This is a crucial part of your answer. It is usually the part that students forget or answer poorly. Just producing a balanced answer is not enough. You have been asked to **evaluate** the extent to which you agree or disagree with the statement '**The General Strike failed because the authorities were more organised than the unions and strikers.**'

It would be easy to sit on the fence and avoid reaching a final conclusion. Sitting on the fence is a dangerous position. Your answer collapses and you lose marks!

Instead, you need to be confident and reach an **overall judgement**.

Here is how to structure a concluding paragraph.

> Start with what you regard as the weaker argument and concede that it still has some strengths.

↓

> Give an example.

↓

> Then make it clear that you think the other argument is stronger.

↓

> Provide your main piece(s) of evidence that support this.

↓

> Try to end with a memorable final sentence.

161

Index

Acknowledgements

The Publisher and authors would like to thank Terry Fiehn for his contribution.

Photo credits

Cover Mary Evans Picture Library; **p.2** © Donald Cumming; **p.5** Kurt Hutton/Picture Post/Getty Images; **p.19** © Centre for the Study of Ancient Documents & The Trustees of the British Museum; **p.22** © 2010 The British Library (ms. Cott. Claud. B.IV 1.59); **p.24** Handschriften und Inkunabel Sammlung. Benediktinerabtei Lambach (Cod. Cml LXXIII f. 64v & 72; **p.27** l Art Archive/Honourable Society of Inner Temple London/Eileen Tweedy, r Roger Coulam/Alamy; **p.32** City of London/HIP/TopFoto; **p.35** t World History Archive/TopFoto, b Mary Evans Picture Library; **p.36** The British Library (Huth 114); **p.41** Photo by Geoff Moore/Rex Features; **p.43** t The British Library/HIP/TopFoto, b Bedfordshire and Luton Archives and Records Service; **p.45** DYLAN MARTINEZ/AFP/Getty Images; **p.50** © The Trustees of the British Museum; **p.56** World History Archive/TopFoto; **p.62** City of London/HIP/TopFoto; **p.64** Museum of London; **p.66** Print Collector/HIP/TopFoto; **p.67** all Mary Evans Picture Library; **p.71** tl Nils Jorgensen/Rex Features, br Today/Rex Features; **p.72** © Aardvark/Alamy; **p.75** Planet News/Popperfoto/Getty Images; **p.76** DYLAN MARTINEZ/AFP/Getty Images; **p.82** © Donald Cumming; **p.86** © Fotomas/TopFoto; **p.88** Museum of London; **p.89** Mary Evans Picture Library; **p.91** l Courtesy of BT Heritage, r Courtesy of Wikimedia Commons; **p.96** tl Museum of London (Henry Grant), tr © Alex Segre/Alamy, b Courtesy of Bryn E. Elliott; **p.97** Michael Stephens/PA News; **p.101** tl Hulton Archive/Getty Images, tr Courtesy of Glasgow Caledonian University Research Collections: The Gallacher Memorial Library, b © Maxton Papers. Licensor www.scran.ac.uk; **p.102** The Granger Collection, NYC/TopFoto; **p.107** Bentley Archive/Popperfoto/Getty Images; **p.108** Mirrorpix; **p.109** Joseph Lee published in the Evening News on 17th November 1939/Solo Syndication/Courtesy of The British Cartoon Archive, University of Kent, www.cartoons.ac.uk; **p.113** Neb [Ronald Niebour] published in the Daily Mail on the 8th May 1950/Solo Syndication/Courtesy of The British Cartoon Archive, University of Kent, www.cartoons.ac.uk; **p.114** Mirrorpix; **p.121** © David Hoffman Photo Library/Alamy; **p.126** t © World History Archive/Alamy, b Topical Press Agency/Hulton Archive/Getty Images; **p.127** Davies/Topical Press Agency/Getty Images; **p.129** © Punch Limited/TopFoto; **p.131** © Mary Evans Picture Library 2008; **p.133** British Library Newspaper Archive; **p.134** Museum of London/HIP/TopFoto; **p.136** © Mary Evans Picture Library 2008; **p.142** © World History Archive/Alamy; **p.144** Kevin KAL Kallaugher, *Today*, Kaltoons.com; **pp.146–147** © Julia Martin Photofusion Picture Library/Alamy; **p.148** t Don McPhee/The Guardian/TopFoto, cr © The Guardian/Alamy, bl © John Harris/reportdigital.co.uk; **p.153** Steve Eason/Hulton Archive/Getty Images; **p.154** Museum of London; **p.157** © Kevin Kallaugher, www.Kaltoons.com; **p.158** Steve Eason/Hulton Archive/Getty Images.

t = top, b = bottom, r = right, l = left

Text extracts

p.38 Douglas Hay, 'Poaching and the game laws on Cannock Chase', in *Albion's Fatal Tree: Crime and Society in Eighteenth-century England*, edited by Douglas Hay, Peter Linebaugh, J. C. Rule, E. P. Thompson and Cal Winslow (Allen Lane, 1975); **p.72** Erwin James, 'Does prison work?', in *The Guardian* (29 January 2001), © Guardian News & Media Ltd 2001; **p.73** John Hoskisson, *Inside: One Man's Experience of Prison* (John Murray, 1998); **p.75** Albert Pierrepoint, *Executioner: Pierrepoint* (Harrap, 1974); **p.77** Intelligence & Security Committee, *Report into the London Terrorist Attacks on 7 July 2005*, © Crown Copyright 2006.

Crown copyright material is reproduced under Class Licence Number CO2P0000060 with the permission of the Controller of HMSO.

Answers to Activity 1, page 68

1727 Mary Mukes and Jane Dennis: Transportation	1891 Annie Cook: Prison (2 days)
1789 Sarah Acton: Transportation	1891 Mary Pulbrook : Prison + 9 months' hard labour
1815 Mary Blake, Elizabeth Smith, Elizabeth Lambert: Death	1700 Rebecca Maud: Death
1837 Mary Dobson: Prison (3 days)	1827 Rosina Smith: Transportation (7 years)
1865 Mary Ann West: Prison 9 months	1674 Mall Floyd: Transportation
	1674 Elizabeth Flower: Branding